Praying *for* Wholeness *and* Healing

RICHARD J. BECKMEN

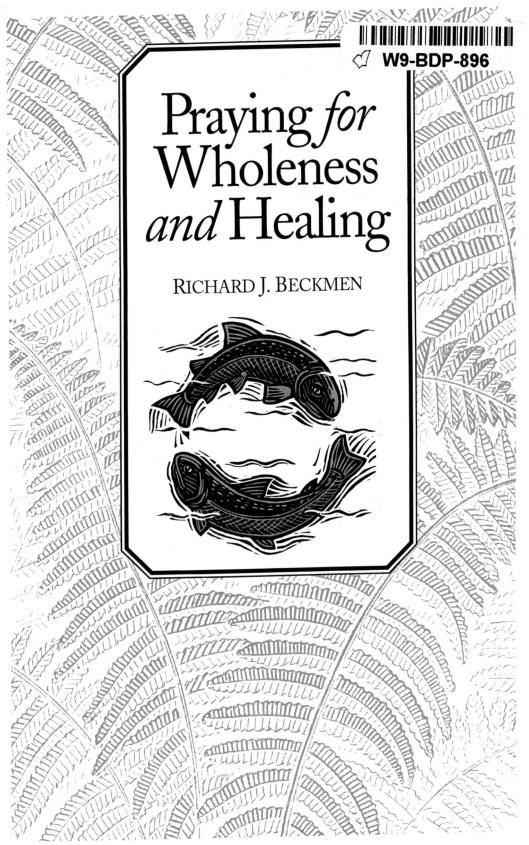

Beckmen, Richard J.
    Praying for wholeness and healing / Richard J. Beckmen.
    80 pp. .635 cm.
    Includes bibliographical references.
    ISBN 0-9744071-0-0
    1. Spiritual Healing. 2. Prayer—Christianity. I. Title.
BT732.5.B367 2003
234'. 13—dc20

The paper used in this publication meets the minimum requirements of American National Standards for Information Sciences— Permanence of Paper for Printed Library Materials, ANSI Z329.48- 1984.

Manufactured in the U.S.A.
1   2   3   4   5   6   7   8   9   10   11   12   13   14   15

CONTENTS

PREFACE

od's gift of prayer is an invitation to seek a face-to-face encounter with God's presence and power. When we pray for healing, we ask God to be a part of the struggle all people share — the search for wholeness in the midst of disease, illness, and brokenness. God, in turn, invites each of us to explore and grow in our understanding of and trust in God's intervention in this struggle. This book will help readers grow in prayer for healing — prayer that will bring God's healing power into our lives and the lives of those for whom we pray.

If you are studying with a group, the following suggestions might be of help to you.

- Remember to pray together as a group and not just talk about prayer.
- Encourage each other to read ahead of time the material you will be discussing and reflect on the questions at the end of the chapter. Encourage personal sharing but share with your group only what is comfortable for you.
- Accept each other where you are in your prayer journey. Everyone is not in the same place. Be open to learning from each other. Be attentive to the questions and struggles others might be having.
- Your group provides a safe and nurturing community in which you can practice praying for healing. Pray for one another and journey together toward the wholeness to which God is calling each of you.

— *Richard J. Beckmen*

About the Cover

The fern is a symbol of piety because ferns grow deep in the forest, not by the highway, so they have to be sought out to be seen. The two trout swim in a circle, incorporating the circle as a universal symbol for wholeness, water as a symbol for baptism, and a fish as a symbol for Christ.

INTRODUCTION

ne of the significant ministries developing in the church today is the ministry of healing through prayer. Growing numbers of congregations are offering healing services with anointing and laying on of hands in the church, at home, or in the hospital.

Pastors and priests have often prayed for healing through their personal ministry with the sick and dying, and the church has been accustomed to providing chaplains at medical facilities. However, there appears to be a renewal of interest in prayer for healing, and churches are rediscovering and broadening the practice of such prayer. Many churches have a prayer chain that prays for requests—many for prayers for healing—from members and friends.

But prayer for healing is now being identified more as a specific ministry of the congregation and one to which lay people might be called. Many denominations have recently published liturgies for healing services, and pastors and lay people are leading these formal services. The charismatic renewal has also led to an increased interest in prayer for healing by calling attention to healing as a spiritual gift or manifestation of the Holy Spirit, as identified in the New Testament (1 Corinthians 12:9, 28).

This book examines the nature of the relationship between prayer and healing. It is intended to encourage congregations and individual Christians to discover the power of prayer for healing and to develop ways this ministry of the church can be enhanced.

The basis for linking prayer and healing lies in the meaning and use of the Greek word for salvation. In several instances after Jesus performs a miracle of healing, he makes the statement, "your faith has saved you," or as it might be translated, "your faith has made you whole or well." In the book, *A Beginner's Guide to Prayer,* I have described the way the word *salvation* related to healing:

> *The Bible uses the word saved not only for being made right with God, but also with reference to the healing of the body. The word for salvation used in the Bible is also the word that is translated made well or whole—the word used when describing the person who has consciously sought healing and is aware that the healing came from God. When disease or illness is overcome in persons without reference to a broad healing that affects the soul or spirit, the word cure is used. When one is cured, a disease and its symptoms are gone, but there is no awareness of a relationship to God in the curing. The word implies a healing or wholeness that occurs when the cure is associated with a relationship with God.*
>
> *In Luke's Gospel, Jesus encounters ten lepers. They appeal to him for healing. He tells them to go and show themselves to the priest. As they go they are cured. One comes back to thank Jesus and acknowledge the healing. Jesus says to the man, "Get up and go on your way; your faith has made you well" (Luke 17:19). A distinction is made between the nine who were cured and the one who was healed, or made well. It is possible to be cured and not healed, according to the New Testament usage of language. Healing refers to the whole person being brought into balance; body, soul, and spirit are brought into a harmony in relationship with God. This does not mean that perfection has been attained. Perfection is not something we will experience in this life. But we experience a sense of well-being when we are at peace with God and others that results in our restored health. The spiritual dimension of healing is important if we are to be healed and not just cured.1*

Even though we tend to think of persons as made up of distinct parts—body, soul, spirit—these parts are merely aspects of one whole person, who is an integrated being with body, soul, and spirit interacting all the time. Jesus' ministry extended to the whole person. What we see happening in the New Testament is a person being physically healed by essentially spiritual means. The opposite—spiritual wholeness being received through physical treatment—can occur, as well, if the person recognizes that healing through physical means is a gift from God. No matter how healing begins, if one aspect of the person is affected, the other parts will also benefit. Jesus did not function with the tools of physical medicine or the techniques of mental and emotional therapy. He used spiritual means to affect persons in all aspects of their being.

In the same way today, Christians use prayer—a spiritual means—to bring about healing. We do not diagnose or treat disease only according to physical medicine or mental health techniques. The instrument of spiritual healing is prayer offered in Jesus' name and with faith that God continues to touch people with healing power and grace to bring wholeness to them. Spiritual healing does not compete with medical science but complements it. God heals in many ways. Healing can come through surgery, drugs, proper diet, counseling—and prayer.

Spiritual healing is important in all our struggles with disease, illness, or disabilities. As long as we are on this earth, we will be less than perfect. There will always be things that are not perfectly right in our bodies, minds, spirits, or relationships. This lack of wholeness can be the source of much discontent, frustration, and anger. We can let it sour our dispositions and turn us into negative, life-denying persons. Or we can claim the imperfection as part of ourselves and become life-affirming and life-giving persons. We can be whole, even if we are not perfect. We can be in a process of being healed in the midst of our illness.

Too often we look for an instantaneous healing that will transform all of our life in one glorious moment. This is not usually what happens. We are on a journey toward wholeness. We experience many forms of healing along the way. Sometimes healing will be physical healing, sometimes psychological, sometimes spiritual, and sometimes relational. We are always moving toward or away from wholeness. If we do not seek healing, we run the risk of losing a part of ourselves. If we ignore a physical symptom, we might get sicker. If we fail to seek forgiveness, we move into spiritual depression or alienation because of guilt.

The why and how of healing remains something of a mystery. We have discovered that certain procedures, drugs, techniques, or prayer will bring about a cure. However, it is not easy to explain why healing occurs. It seems to be built into us at an unknowable level. As Christians we could even say that God has built a natural healing process into creation. In addition, many New Testament writers describe the saving work of Jesus in broad terms, proclaiming that the whole creation is being drawn to wholeness in Christ Jesus. God's goal for creation seems to be complete restoration and reconciliation for all things. The following scripture passages reflect this view.

For in him all the fullness of God was pleased to dwell, and through him God was pleased to reconcile to himself all things, whether on earth or in heaven, by making peace through the blood of his cross. (Colossians 1:19-20)

I consider that the sufferings of this present time are not worth comparing with the glory about to be revealed to us. For the creation waits with eager longing for the revealing of the children of God; for the creation was subjected to futility, not of its own will but by the will of the one who subjected it, in hope that the creation itself will be set free from its bondage to decay and will obtain the freedom of the glory of the children of God.   *(Romans 8:18-21)*

May the God of peace himself sanctify you entirely; and may your spirit and soul and body be kept sound and blameless at the coming of our Lord Jesus Christ. The one who calls you is faithful, and he will do this.
(1 Thessalonians 5:23-24)

In the midst of the human struggle with sin, sickness, brokenness, and death, the Christian community seeks to bear witness to the saving work of Jesus Christ, who is Lord. The lordship of Jesus Christ extends to every aspect of human life and brings the power of God to bear on each point of struggle. Like a down payment from God on the future glory, signs of Jesus' lordship appear among us in the forgiving, healing, and consoling we experience through the work of the Holy Spirit.

As we study prayer and healing, we can keep in mind this underlying truth that supports the Christian in all aspects of ministry: Jesus Christ is Lord, and he desires to give life and to give it abundantly. God is at work, constantly seeking to be present to this world through his people, so that all things may be restored in God and all things may reflect God's glory.

For REFLECTION *and* DISCUSSION

1. Remember a time when you experienced healing in your body. Reflect on a particular disease, pain, or wound. Try to recall how healing happened. What process of healing did you experience?

2. How comfortable are you with the idea that a spiritual exercise like prayer can effect a cure? What questions does that thought raise in you?

ACTIVITY

If you or someone you know has any physical, emotional, relational, or spiritual illness, begin to pray each day for the illness to be healed. Take time to relax before you pray, and devote some specific, focused time to this prayer.

Chapter One

A CHRISTIAN VIEW *of* SPIRITUAL HEALING

I came that they may have life, and have it abundantly.
(John 10:10)

od is for us and not against us. God desires that all taste the bread of life, drink the living water, which is Jesus.

The gospel is good news for the poor, the sick, the outcast, the demon possessed, and all who suffer. The gospel is good news for the sinner, the tortured one, the guilt laden, and the fearful. Jesus came proclaiming the kingdom of God, God's reign among humans, and he performed signs that supported his teaching and preaching. Chief among those signs was healing. It is difficult to read the Bible and not see the role that healing plays in God's revelation of love and power for all of creation. Having created a finite and mortal human being, subject to sin, sickness, and death, God does not abandon humans. The biblical story recounts God's activity to reconcile, redeem, and reclaim all in creation.

This reconciling and healing work of God for all creation became focused in the life and ministry of Jesus. Jesus healed all kinds of disease—physical ills, demon possession, sin, alienation—that affected all aspects of human life. He brought this salvation through his ministry of preaching, teaching, and healing. He established it as an ongoing gift in his death and resurrection. From that gift, the Holy Spirit leads the church to continue to preach, teach, and heal in the power of God.

Basic Affirmations on Healing

What basic affirmations can be made about healing today in the Christian community?

- All healing comes from God, no matter what form that healing takes. Therefore, there should not be a competitive spirit between the church and the medical community. Medical practices should not be rejected by Christians who desire to use only prayer for treatment. Those who reject medicine are rejecting gifts—medical research and practice—that God has given us.
- A ministry of praying for healing is a part of the Christian church's regular ministry.
- The healing ministry of the gospel is present in the church where the Word is proclaimed, sins confessed and forgiven, the sacraments practiced, and the fellowship of Christians experienced in mutual encouragement and prayer support. All of these practices in the church are vehicles of healing.
- The ministry of healing prayer in the church is a ministry to the whole person. Spiritual healing, or healing through prayer, describes the method of the healing but is not confined to spiritual concerns. That is, we can receive spiritual healing for sickness of the human spirit, as well as for sicknesses that affect the body, mind, emotions, and relationships.
- The ministry of praying for healing is a ministry of the whole congregation. Even though certain individuals carry out the ministry, it is on behalf of the congregation that this ministry is done.

Healing and God's Will

Is it God's will to heal? Before we can answer this question, we need to discuss the source of illness, disease, and sickness. Is God the author of sickness? There are indications in the Old Testament that this was a view held by some. In Deuteronomy, the following curse would come upon those who disobeyed God's commandments:

The Lord will afflict you with consumption, fever, inflammation, with fiery heat and drought, and with blight and mildew; they shall pursue you until you perish.
(Deuteronomy 28:22)

Jesus' disciples ask him, "Who sinned, this man or his parents, that he was born blind?" (John 9:2). This question implies an understanding that there is a direct relationship between a particular sin and sickness, and that the sickness is a punishment for sin. Jesus responds (in contrast to Old Testament thinking) by saying, "Neither this man nor his parents sinned; he was born blind so that

God's works might be revealed in him" (John 9:3). Jesus is saying that God's work is in the healing, not in the creation of sickness as judgment.

There are some who also say that God sends sickness as a trial to strengthen faith or test the mettle of the children God created. But God does not work against God's self-expressed work of healing and restoring.

Although God does not cause suffering, there are times when following God's will involves suffering, The most dramatic example of this is when Jesus prayed in the Garden of Gethsemane before his crucifixion. "Father, if you are willing, remove this cup from me; yet, not my will but yours be done" (Luke 22:42). Jesus requested another option from God, if it was God's will. But it was not God's will to offer another option, so Jesus walked the road of passion to suffering and death. The struggle in the garden was between God's will and Jesus' desire. In the end, Jesus surrendered to God's will and took the path of voluntary suffering. When he followed God's will, Jesus also experienced God's care and ultimate victory in the resurrection.

Voluntary suffering is often part of the Christian walk. Jesus said that we are to take up our cross and follow him. He also spoke of the times when we would experience persecution because we follow him. Obedience to the will of God can lead us to suffering—rejection, ridicule, even stonings, burnings, and the like.

Involuntary suffering is suffering that comes to us without our choosing it. It is the suffering that comes from disease, accident, and calamity. It is God's will to stand with us against those forces—forces outside God and outside ourselves—that create suffering. In each particular case, God will be with us, whether or not we eventually experience a cure.

Even though I have learned much about the source of suffering and God's desire to heal us, in the midst of praying for healing for someone, I will still sometimes find myself wondering, *Is it God's will to heal?* The answer that comes most often to mind is the story of the blind man sitting by the roadside outside Jericho. He hears that Jesus of Nazareth is passing by. He calls out loudly for Jesus to have mercy on him. The crowd tries to silence him. He calls out even more. Jesus hears him and asks that the man be brought to him. When he is brought forward, Jesus asks an open-ended question: "What do you want me to do for you?" (Luke 18:35ff). The man asks for healing, and Jesus restores his sight.

Jesus' question is neither capricious nor cruel. Jesus would not have asked the question if it were not God's will that the man be healed. In the same way, Jesus would not ask his disciples to go out to preach, teach, and heal if this ministry were not God's will (see Matthew 10:1-15). Although we might at times in effect choose suffering by choosing to do God's will, we can in the end say with confidence, yes, it is God's will that all creation should be healed.

Our Image of God and Praying for Healing

How we pray and what we pray for are related to how we think of God. If we picture God as an angry and spiteful being, it will be difficult for us to feel that we can properly ask God for anything. If we imagine God as a hard-driving, bossy deity who is always demanding perfection, we might find it impossible to pray in freedom and honesty. If we think of God as an enemy, we will hardly dare ask for anything good.

How do we think about God?

Whoever has seen me has seen the Father. How can you say, "Show us the Father"? Do you not believe that I am in the Father and the Father is in me? The words that I say to you I do not speak on my own; but the Father who dwells in me does his works. (John 14:9-10)

Jesus says that we know God when we know him; we hear God's word to us when we listen to what Jesus says; we see the works of God when we see what Jesus does.

What do we know about Jesus that reveals God? What do we hear from him? What do we see in his works?

Often circumstances seem to deny God's goodness, but Jesus reveals a compassionate God who is on our side. In Jesus we see a God who is present to us. Jesus came to see us, to hear us, to be near us, and to let us experience the nearness of God.

In Jesus we know a caring God. Jesus' works manifest the power of God to love, to heal, to forgive, and to reconcile. We are God's children, and God cares deeply about us, the ones God has made and redeemed in Christ.

God is with us because God loves us. Christian prayers for healing are offered to God through this relationship we have in our Lord Jesus Christ. And it is out of this relationship that we know how and what to pray when we intercede for those in need of healing.

For REFLECTION *and* DISCUSSION

1. How do you respond to the five basic affirmations listed in this chapter? Do you agree with them? Why or why not?

2. In what ways do you believe God's will and healing are related?

3. Does your image of God fit with the picture of God that emerges in this chapter? How is it similar or different?

4. Reflect on a time when you felt God was calling you to face a situation that would lead to voluntary suffering. How did you respond? In what ways did you experience God's grace in that situation?

ACTIVITIES

1. Take an informal poll among your friends. Ask them if they believe that it is God's will to heal people through prayer. Discuss with them their reasons for believing as they do.

2. As you have opportunity, ask your doctor what he or she thinks about spiritual healing. Does your doctor pray for patients? Why or why not? Has your doctor had any experiences that relate to spiritual healing?

3. Write a brief list of affirmations or presuppositions you think you can make about healing through prayer.

Chapter Two

The ROLE of PRAYER in HEALING

"And now, Lord, look at their threats, and grant to your servants to speak your word with all boldness, while you stretch out your hand to heal, and signs and wonders are performed through the name of your holy servant Jesus." When they had prayed, the place in which they were gathered together was shaken; and they were all filled with the Holy Spirit and spoke the word of God with boldness.
(Acts 4:29-31)

rom the beginning, the Christian community understood itself as a community that was called to pray. Through prayer, the community found itself imbued with God's presence, motivated to serve, and encouraged to act out its faith in works of mercy, witness, and power.

Prayerfulness

Prayerfulness is the state of consciously walking with God through life. Prayerfulness is not so much the act of saying prayers, although that is part of it, as it is living in the awareness of God's presence. This is the goal toward which most serious Christians strive. Yet being prayerful is one of the most difficult disciplines for the Christian to maintain.

This difficulty is especially pronounced in our contemporary society. We live too fast, seek too much, and concern ourselves with too many other goals. Seriously distracted by our many pursuits, we find ourselves pulled in any number of directions at once. It becomes difficult for us to be still, focused, and attentive to God—commitments we need to make in order to be prayerful people. This makes it difficult for us to listen to God—to hear the still small voice with which God speaks. Our scatteredness also makes it difficult for us to be aware of those around us, to see them through the eyes of Christ, and to relate to them at a deep level.

In order to become prayerful, we need to begin placing prayer near the top of our list of priorities. Becoming a channel of God's healing presence is a process. It means seeking a relationship with God that is open, confident, and familiar—a process that for today might mean bringing to God our doubt, fear, hesitation, anger, and confusion.

Prayerfulness is a description of a relationship rather than a description of an activity, although the relationship will be expressed in activity, such as prayer. The images that Jesus used to describe the relationship between the pray-er and God are images that reflect intimacy, caring, and trust.

Jesus used a variety of images to describe his—and our—relationship with God. In John 15 Jesus describes the intimate relationship between himself, God, and the believer using the image of the vine and the branches. It is a living, dynamic, shared relationship characterized by abiding in one another through love and obedience. Jesus also often used the image of a heavenly father. It is the opening image of the Lord's Prayer. He used it again in Luke when he described God as a father more loving and caring than any human:

> *If you then, who are evil, know how to give good gifts to your children, how much more will the heavenly Father give the Holy Spirit to those who ask him!*
> *(Luke 11:13)*

In the Gospels Jesus often expressed his relationship with God by praying before he made major decisions. Jesus told the disciples at his ascension to go to Jerusalem and wait. The disciples interpreted that word *wait* to mean that they should be in prayer. The fruit of their waiting was that they were ready to receive the gift of the Holy Spirit on Pentecost. Throughout the Book of Acts, the disciples prayed before major decisions. Prayerfulness accompanied them in all their doings.

Praying for healing was one of the ways Jesus' disciples—including his twentieth century disciples—express their walk with God in Christ. This ministry is based on what we see and hear while walking with Jesus. Prayerfulness is not just a goal for the individual Christian. It is a goal for any congregation or fellowship of believers. As a church sets a priority on prayerfulness, it opens itself to become a powerful instrument of ministry and mission.

Prayerfulness and Healing

Praying for healing in a spirit of prayerfulness means being open to respond to God and the situation. Prayerfulness is as much listening for God's direction as it is speaking to God on behalf of another person. Prayerfulness is that ongoing walk with God through which we become more fit vessels for God's healing power to touch another person.

Agnes Sanford, a well-known teacher of healing prayer, describes in a simple way what it means to link prayer and healing out of a spirit of prayerfulness. Three simple statements sum up the process. "The first step in seeking to produce results by any power is to contact that power … .The second step is to turn it on … .The third step is to believe that this power is coming into use and to accept it by faith. No matter how much we ask for something it becomes ours only as we accept it and give thanks for it."[2]

The first step in Agnes Sanford's description of the healing process is what I have been describing as prayerfulness. The second step might be referred to as the act of prayer or request for healing. For the person seeking healing, this step means turning the desire to be healed into an active request for one's own healing, or asking someone else to pray for that healing.

If we are asked to pray for someone, although Sanford describes this step as turning on the power, we need to understand that we ourselves are not the power, the healer. God is always the one who heals. To pray for healing is to seek to be a channel of God's healing presence and love. Although we will never be able to do it perfectly, it is important that we seek to maintain this attitude when praying for healing. The focus is not on us. We are not on trial in this act of praying. The outcome is not dependent on us. We do not need to be preoccupied with ourselves. Our goal, rather, is to focus only on God and the other person, clinging to God's promises in Christ and bringing before God in a spirit of compassion the one for whom we are praying. We seek to be an open window through which the breath of the Holy Spirit may blow upon this person. In the prayer of faith, we lose ourselves in the ocean of God's healing grace and mercy.

The third step is to receive what God gives and to give thanks for it. This means acknowledging and acting on the results of the prayer. It is good to verbalize this thanksgiving when we are praying with someone and to acknowledge that God has heard the prayer and is answering it. Giving thanks for healing is not a matter of saying *how* God is answering the prayer but simply *that* God is answering it. The specific results might never be known to us.

Three different types of prayer are involved in this process. The *prayer of the heart*, that deep meditational prayer that seeks to know the loving presence of God, becomes aware of God's love and power. The *prayer of faith* acts in trust on the promises of God to pray specifically for what is needed. The *prayer of gratitude* acknowledges that God is answering and receives the wholeness God is giving.

No matter what type of prayer we offer, we want to remember that to pray is not to dominate. We do not need to think of ourselves as taking charge of someone when we pray for him or her to be healed. We do not need to direct either God or the person for whom we are praying. When we pray, we become a servant. The prayerful intercessor serves both God's will and the needs of the sick person. We place ourselves alongside the needy one and share in compassion with him or her and wait for God's hand to touch and bless.

Although all of us will become more prayerful as our relationship with God grows, even those intercessors who are most aware of God's presence in their prayer will discover that the experience of healing is varied. There is no single prayer formula. Sometimes a simple prayer is all that is needed. Hezekiah cried for the Lord to heal him, and he was healed.

Other times healing is a longer process and the prayer might extend for quite a period of time. A young woman with cancer came regularly to our healing service over the course of several months while she was also being treated medically. Various kinds of prayer accompanied her on her healing journey. These prayers included laying on of hands, anointing with oil, several people gathering around her for extended prayer periods, requests made to a telephone prayer chain, her own prayers, and prayers from her family. The cancer was treated and cured. Today she describes the experience of being healed as a long process of being made whole in body and spirit. She also speaks of the prayerfulness that developed in her own life and that actually seemed to surround her because of the prayers of others.

Prayerfulness can also grow in the one praying, providing the pray-er with the awareness he or she needs to listen to God, as well as to the person who comes seeking healing. Prayerfulness sometimes leads to important insights into the situation at hand. For example, on occasion the one who is praying might become aware that God is healing at that very moment. I remember several occasions when someone who came to a service for healing was healed as he or she knelt and received an anointing. Our prayer at that point was not that God would heal this person. Rather, we offered a prayer of thanksgiving for God's healing.

Prayerfulness is being attentive to the leading of God, so that we are responding to God and to the person we are with. Sometimes, for example, when a person comes to receive prayers for healing, seeking a cure for some illness, the prayerful intercessor becomes aware that there are other issues that need healing as well. The one praying can reframe the prayers to include these needs. I remember a man who came seeking prayers to bring quietness and contentment to him. He thought he had an emotional problem. After a period of discernment and guidance, we determined that the root of the problem was a spiritual one having to do with some sins he was not facing in his life. Once these were prayed for, he found the peace he was seeking.

As we become more prayerful, consciously aware of walking in God's presence, we will discover greater opportunities to serve. We will see human need more clearly. And we will have more confidence in God's desire and power to act through us.

Healing Prayer and Scientific Research

From time to time scientific studies have been conducted to determine the effects of prayer on sickness. The studies are difficult to conduct and have often been ignored by most of the medical community. However, at the same time as there is renewed interest in healing prayer by the church, members of the scientific community have been conducting studies and writing about the implications of those studies. A recent book, *Healing Words* by Larry Dossey, M.D., takes another look at most of the studies, both past and present.

The church has not necessarily looked to the scientific community to establish the credibility of prayer for healing. In fact, Dossey himself makes that observation.

> *To be sure, prayer does not need science to legitimate or justify it. Even so, I believe that if science can demonstrate the potency of prayer, people who pray are likely to feel empowered and validated in their belief as a result. Furthermore, using science does not always require that we "put nature on the rack" and torture her to reveal her secrets, to use Bacon's images. Instead we can honor what is being investigated and approach it with respect and reverence. From this point of view, investigating prayer does not imply "bringing God into the laboratory" but "bringing the laboratory to God," requesting and inviting the Universe to reveal its workings.[3]*

As we read the reports of these studies, there seems to be evidence in them that prayer does have an effect, as viewed from a scientific perspective. Because such tests are non-repeatable, it is difficult to provide the kind of data expected in a scientific experiment. However, it appears that the medical community might be more open to exploring the role of prayer in healing and be more willing to advocate its use. For those who have an interest in this subject and who might themselves be in the medical community, I would recommend reading *Healing Words* and other such works that explore the evidence for a relationship between prayer and curing.

For REFLECTION *and* DISCUSSION

1. What are your particular struggles in living prayerfully? What draws you away from consciously living each day in an awareness of God's presence?

2. Review the three steps in praying for healing described by Agnes Sanford. Does this process suggest any changes you might want to make in the way you pray for healing? What are they?

3. Would scientific evidence of a positive relationship between prayer and healing affect the way you pray for healing? In what ways would this change your attitudes or practice?

ACTIVITIES

1. If prayerfulness is attentiveness to God in your daily walk, attempt to develop some disciplines that will help you remember this. Seek this discipline in a spirit of gentleness; that is, pay attention to your own rhythms and circumstances and experiment to find disciplines that work best for you. You could set a specific time each day to meditate; carry a reminder of prayerfulness in your pocket, such as a small cross or other symbol; or pray a brief prayer each hour on the hour.

2. Find ways to use for yourself and others these prayer blessings: see Romans 15:13; 2 Corinthians 13:13; Ephesians 6:23; 1 Thessalonians 5:23; 2 Thessalonians 3:16; Hebrews 13:20-21. You could use one for a week, and then choose another for the following week. Notice how these blessings affect your experience each day.

3. If the scientific testing of the relationship between prayer and healing interests you, continue to read and to explore that topic. (See For Further Reading, page 79, for possible resources.)

Chapter Three

FAITH *and* HEALING

"Lord, I believe; help my unbelief."
(Mark 9:24)

The honest man who came to Jesus and asked him to heal
his son spoke the words above. He revealed the dilemma
that confronts most people who pray for healing—the tension between doubt and faith.

Faith is present when healing happens. Throughout the Bible the
accounts of healing often make reference to the fact that faith is present. Faith
is not the same as wish fulfillment or a flight of fantasy. It is not invoking some
sort of magical incantation or rite that will in and of itself produce a miracle.
Faith is not the supreme exercise of the human will to maximize its power.
Faith, as described in the Bible, is seen as acting in trust based on the evidence
of God's promise or actions in the past. Faith is rooted in the conviction that
God does act in human affairs and responds to human need.

Early in his ministry Jesus took the initiative to heal people. As people
heard about his ability to heal, they began to come to him. They called and
reached out to him so they could experience for themselves what he had done
for others. The witness of those he healed led others to hope. Their hope was
expressed in the belief that Jesus could do the same for them. He did not disappoint them but made them well.

We read already in the first chapter of Mark's Gospel that Jesus cast out a
demon from a young boy. The story ends with the statement, "At once [Jesus']
fame began to spread throughout the surrounding region of Galilee" (Mark
1:28). Word spread quickly and inspired many who came to Jesus, trusting in
his power to make them well.

Shortly after this incident, Jesus was teaching in a house in Capernaum. A
great crowd had gathered in and out of the house. Four men came carrying a

paralyzed friend. They climbed to the roof and made an opening and lowered the sick man in front of Jesus. Jesus healed the man, telling him to get up and take his stretcher and go home. The four men who brought the paralytic acted in faith. It was a dramatic, acted-out prayer for healing. Having heard about Jesus, they brought their friend in faith, trusting that he could be healed. And Jesus did not disappoint them.

Faith, given by the Holy Spirit, grows in the light of testimony to God's mighty acts. Such testimony invites us to trust what God can do. We might doubt, as did the father of the epileptic child (See Mark 9:14-29. Note that the man believed and risked acting on that belief, even in the face of his doubt). No matter how great our doubt, however, by immersing ourselves in Scripture and the witness of the contemporary church about healing, the Holy Spirit can give us faith to pray for healing.

Because we all experience both doubt and faith, it is important if we intend to pray for healing that we continually nurture our faith. Scripture study and reflection, along with significant time spent in prayer, are important for the pray-er. When we see Jesus, for example, at work in his healing ministry, our faith is strengthened by the Holy Spirit, increasing our openness to and expectation for healing. This is important because the healing that happens is not based on our faith alone but on what faith sees as the work of God.

In addition, knowing Scripture allows us to share stories about Christ's healing with those for whom we are praying, so that they also can be encouraged to believe.

When Jesus stood before the tomb of Lazarus, he lifted his eyes to heaven and prayed. The Gospel writer tells us that Jesus did this not for his own sake but for the sake of those who were watching. He was confident that God would raise Lazarus. He wanted those who stood by to know that it was by the power of God that Lazarus would come forth from the grave. He wanted them to know so that they would have faith.

The Source of Healing

In James, a passage about healing links prayer and faith:

Are any among you suffering? They should pray. Are any cheerful? They should sing songs of praise. Are any among you sick? They should call for the elders of the church and have them pray over them, anointing them with oil in the name of the Lord. The prayer of faith will save the sick, and the Lord will raise them up . . . .
(James 5:13–15)

In order not to place a burden on ourselves or others, we want to be clear about the source of healing. It is not faith that heals, although faith is present when healing happens. God heals. As James says, " ... and the Lord will raise them up ... " (v. 15). Faith reaches out to God and expects and receives with thanksgiving whatever God gives but does not produce or control what is given.

A story in Mark describes an experience Jesus had in Nazareth. People in his hometown rejected Jesus when he came and preached in their synagogue.

And he could do no deed of power there, except that he laid his hands on a few sick people and cured them. And he was amazed at their unbelief.

(Mark 6:5)

In spite of the unbelief of that community, Jesus healed. Our faith does not control Jesus and healing can happen without it, but nevertheless faith becomes the instrument through which we see what Jesus can do. Faith opens us to healing for ourselves and others.

So faith has a foundation in the witness of what God has done and can do. Our faith is nurtured by this testimony, and by it we are encouraged as the eyes of the heart are enlightened by God's Spirit (Ephesians 1:18) to see the power of God at work.

Faith and Action

Action is another important characteristic of faith that relates to healing prayer. As we are encouraged to believe that God desires to heal, we take steps to act on that belief. Our faith becomes more than a deeply held conviction. We are challenged to risk acting on that conviction. Every time I move to pray for healing, I am aware that there is an inner resistance to that action. My resistance is rooted in the realization that I am risking something by acting on a promise, and that I have no guarantee I can accomplish anything in my own power. I might also be feeling afraid that I am not worthy to pray. Whatever the causes, there is this sense of risk involved. It is at this point that the Holy Spirit prods and pulls me to act, in spite of barriers that are present.

The element of risk involved in asking for healing is illustrated in the story of the woman who was hemorrhaging and came to Jesus. She had been suffering for years and had used up all of her money. Doctors were unable to help her. She had heard about Jesus' power to heal, so she worked her way through the crowd and touched his cloak, " ... for she said, 'If I but touch his clothes, I will be made well' " (Mark 5:28). Notice the progression in this story. Faith was stirred as the woman recalled what she had heard about Jesus. She went to where he was and reached out to touch his garments. She believed and acted on her faith.

The woman's behavior is remarkable when you consider that she was acting against very strong taboos and social restrictions. Jewish women did not touch strange men in public. Even more, because she was hemorrhaging she was considered unclean and was not supposed to touch or be touched by anyone. In spite of these barriers, she acted on her faith and was made well. Her faith and actions were rewarded in several ways. Jesus, when he discovered who had touched him, did not reprimand or embarrass her because she stepped out of bounds. He called her "daughter"—an endearing and embracing phrase. Then he sent her on her way, healed and at peace.

The woman acted in faith but at the same time tried to act secretly. Because of her circumstances she was discreet but, nevertheless, bold. Sometimes it is necessary to be quite bold. In Luke 18:35-43, a blind beggar revealed a radical faith. As Jesus was passing by with a crowd, the blind man asked who was coming. Hearing that it was Jesus, he began to shout for Jesus to help him. The crowd tried to silence him sternly. But he shouted even louder. When he heard the man, Jesus asked that he be brought forward. Jesus then asked him a question, "What do you want me to do for you?" The beauty of the question lies in its openness, in the opportunity it provides for the blind man to express his faith. The blind man responded, "Lord, let me see again." Jesus responded, "Receive your sight; your faith has saved you." Immediately the man received his sight, and he followed Jesus singing the praises of God.

When Jesus saw his disciples being intimidated by circumstances, he chided them for their lack of faith. Faith is the window that opens us to God's blessings—the blessings of healing, strength, confidence, and consolation. The faith that acts is the faith that receives these blessings. Faith has the eyes to see the moment of opportunity, but faith also has the courage to seize that moment.

Praying for healing is a bold act. Social, spiritual, or emotional barriers might arise in our minds. Do I have authority to do this? What will people think? Is this appropriate? What if nothing happens? Fear might set in and cause us to shrink back from praying. In those situations it is helpful to remember stories like the woman with the hemorrhage, or the blind beggar, or the countless others who stepped through the fear with courage to act.

Compassion and Righteousness

Compassion is a significant motivator for the faith to act. Time after time, Jesus is described as looking at someone, being moved by compassion, and healing that person. This compassion is the love that prompted God to send his Son. This compassion is the love that responds to the needs of another. The prayer of faith becomes a channel of love through which we offer ourselves as a vehicle for God's love to touch the one for whom we pray. Focused totally on the sick one whom God loves, compassion prompts us to pray in faith and to claim the grace-filled promise of God.

When we become intimidated by such diseases as AIDS or certain forms of cancer that do not have a positive prognosis, we can pray for the gift of compassion, so that in faith we might be freed to pray, with openness toward God's blessing. Again we read in James, " … pray for one another, so that you may be healed" (James 5:16). This strong admonition to seek healing is followed by the assurance, "The prayer of the righteous [the one who has a right relationship with God] is powerful and effective."

This verse is from a larger passage in James that reflects the early church's continuing healing ministry as an expression of the compassion of God. It is assumed that the people of the church—people of compassion—will also be righteous and capable of praying in faith, that is, praying with trust that God will act and claiming God's promises for healing.

Persistence

Faith is a response to the promise of God. It clings to the promise, even when circumstances would seem to say that healing is not possible. This is the steadfastness of faith. This aspect of faith is important when praying for healing, since most often healing is a process that takes time. When prayers for healing are first offered, some people might get worse before they begin to get better. Faith needs to continue believing and praying. Faith looks to the promise of God and not just at the circumstances. Faith is not like a barometer that responds to changes in air pressure and has no reading of its own. Faith is constant in the midst of change, for better or for worse, so that prayer can always be focused on the steadfast manifestation of God's glory in whatever blessing God bestows.

In the Gospel of John, we read the story of Jesus raising Lazarus from the dead. Mary and Martha had sent for Jesus when Lazarus became ill. Jesus delayed his coming and Lazarus died. Mary and Martha were distraught because Jesus had not arrived in time. Understandably, Mary and Martha were focused on Lazarus' death and assumed that his life was over. When Jesus came and asked that the grave be opened, Martha objected, saying that Lazarus had been dead four days. Jesus said to her, "Did I not tell you that if you believed, you would see the glory of God?" (John 11:40).

Faith opens the window on God's grace so that God's glory is revealed in the midst of this world. Faith in its radical persistence seeks to be an instrument of God's grace and love. Having experienced forgiveness and reconciliation, healing and renewal, the person of faith turns to the broken world and takes up the ministry of healing. The person of faith prays, seeking to be a channel of God's love. The person of faith prays, knowing that God will enfold the pain, suffering, and hurt of others with consoling and healing love. This is a work of faith.

For REFLECTION *and* DISCUSSION

1. How do you respond when you feel doubt, especially with regard to prayer and healing? What do you doubt about God? What do you doubt about yourself?

2. What evidence, as a foundation to faith, comes to mind when you think about or engage in prayers for healing? Do you turn to Scripture? Experience? Are there specific stories or images that provide a foundation for you?

3. What intimidates you when you think about or offer prayers for healing? Do you doubt whether you have authority to do what you are doing? Do you tend to focus on the power of the disease you are confronting, or on your own weakness and vulnerability as a human? Do you think about the risk of trying something that might not work? Or are there other things that make you reluctant to pray for healing?

ACTIVITIES

1. Ask your pastor or a lay hospital visitor if you could accompany him or her on a hospital visit and join in offering prayers for healing for that person.

2. If you are uncomfortable praying aloud in the presence of others, ask a family member or close friend if you may pray for him or her. Begin with laying on of hands and silent prayers, and then offer simple oral prayers as you feel moved to do so. If there is no specific illness to pray for, offer a prayer for general health and well-being. Continue this practice until you feel comfortable praying aloud.

Chapter Four

FORGIVENESS *and* HEALING

"Which is easier, to say to the paralytic, 'Your sins are forgiven,'
or to say, 'Stand up and take your mat and walk'?"
(Mark 2:9)

ometimes it is difficult to know what is really important in healing. We can easily be impressed by the seeming miraculous in a physical healing. But is such healing really more significant than the spiritual healing found in forgiveness?

From a biblical point of view, the forgiveness of sins is the deepest and most significant healing we can receive. Forgiveness of sins is the healing that restores our relationship with God.

It is hard to imagine anything more tragic than human beings separated from their Creator. Having a relationship with God that is positive, life giving, and open means knowing peace and contentment at its deepest. Humans have been made for life with God. As the apostle Paul said in his sermon in Athens, "In him we live and move and have our being" (Acts 17:28). To be cut off from God is to be cut off from the source of life, the wisdom of life, the meaning of life. To be separated from God is to live in spiritual blindness. Being separated from God means thinking we can make it without God—or thinking we have no value in God's eyes. Being separated from God is sin, which puts us under the threat of condemnation and creates in us a sense of guilt that gives birth to fear and violence.

The problem we face is that sin is present in every one of us humans. It is a condition that distorts what God has created and turns us in upon ourselves so that we serve, not the one who created us, but ourselves and other parts of the creation. What has been affected is the deepest part of us—the spiritual dimension of our lives. This spiritual part of us most significantly defines who we are: children of God.

God's Reconciliation

The major theme of the Bible is the story of God seeking to reconcile us to God's own self. It is the story of a seeking, wooing, calling Creator who desires to bring the whole family together into a community of joy, harmony, and love. It is the story of God taking the initiative to do for us what we cannot do for ourselves, in order that we may come home to our Maker.

God offered to the world the gift of Jesus Christ. For those who believe in Jesus as God's Son and confess their sinfulness and sins to him, God does forgive and offers all the benefits of being a child of God. These benefits bring life and sensitivity to our spiritual selves so that we may be alive to God, open to God's Word, responsive to God's Spirit, and free from sin, fear, guilt, and all their negative results in our lives.

Why is forgiveness so important to healing? Some years ago I was visiting a chaplain at the state mental institution in North Dakota. What he told me that day has deeply influenced me. He contended that over half of the patients at the hospital were there because of the preaching of the church at that time. He found these people laden with guilt from which they could not free themselves. They knew they were sinners and separated from God in their spirit. This was the message they heard Sunday after Sunday. The message they did not hear—sometimes because it was not preached—was that God forgives sin with no conditions attached through the gift of Jesus Christ. Their guilt became so great that it brought them emotional, mental, and spiritual sickness so serious that they could not face life, themselves, God, or others. They needed to know that they were loved and forgiven by God.

We hear as well in the Bible the cry of the alienated, the lonely voice of people caught in guilt. In Psalm 32 the psalmist describes a time in his life when he was in such a condition.

Confessing our sin and receiving forgiveness is the most powerful healing instrument there is. It provides a foundational healing through God's mercy that opens the door of our heart, mind, will, and feelings to the presence and love of God. That love from God is the key to all healing and the key to the power of all who would be a channel of God's healing for others through prayer.

Because sin has such a persistent hold on us, frequent confession is important for those who pray for healing in others. The freeing power of forgiveness enables us to pray with confidence, not because we are sinless but because we are forgiven. Experiencing and understanding God's mercy allows us to pray with boldness and declare with conviction God's love for others.

Dealing with Guilt

Many persons who come to us for prayers for healing will be bound in fear, anger, and frustration. Their problems might well have their roots in the person's unwillingness or inability to let go of guilt. Or the problems might be present because the person has failed—for whatever reason—to forgive another. It is difficult for us to let go of our guilt. Many people hold on even though they go through the act of confession. They do not appropriate God's mercy or their status as a forgiven child of God. Their guilt might well prevent them from seeing that they can be healed—physically and mentally, as well as spiritually. It is appropriate when praying for such people to ask God to help them let go of their guilt.

When we pray face to face with people for them to be healed, we might encounter, on the other hand, some who desire to share very personal accounts of their sins. They might unburden themselves quite openly. We need to recognize this as a time of private confession and receive what they say, simply acknowledging to them that we are listening. This is not a time to excuse them, make rationalizations for what they did, or try to convince them that they are good people. And by all means this is not the time to probe for further details about the matter they are confessing. (Remember, too, that they have trusted us with personal information. That is to be shared with no one. This is true of all information people share with us when they come seeking prayers for healing.) Confession is a voluntary act. People will share what they want and are able to share. They will share in trust that we will hear them and provide assurance of God's forgiveness and mercy for them. And indeed, we are present to be a channel for God's forgiving love, not to be an accuser, judge, or savior. Christ has died for them, Satan has no power to accuse them, and God forgives them for Jesus' sake. A simple assurance of God's mercy, a reminder of Christ's death on the cross for them, and a prayer of thanksgiving and encouragement are all that are needed. The Holy Spirit will do the rest.

It is particularly important for those who are intercessors to live with a lively sense of forgiveness. When we pray for healing but do not have a sense of being forgiven, it is difficult for us to pray about and communicate God's mercy and forgiveness. We might end up projecting our own situation on those for whom we are praying, reinforcing their resistance to accepting and living in forgiveness.

Forgiveness is the foundation for all healing. Forgiveness is the foundation for the confidence we have to pray for healing of all sorts. Therefore we will want to enjoy daily the experience of God's mercy through confession and forgiveness. Through this experience we can be the most effective channels possible for God's love and mercy.

For REFLECTION *and* DISCUSSION

1. Reflect on your own experience of being forgiven. What is it like for you when you experience forgiveness, as opposed to your experience of life under guilt or shame?

2. What obstacles do you encounter that block either your confession of sin or your sense of being forgiven?

3. What has been your experience of forgiveness as healing? What was healed in that experience?

4. Reflect on James 5:13-16. How do you imagine this passage being lived out in your congregation?

ACTIVITIES

1. Reflect on and discuss with others how you would converse with and pray for someone who seemed stuck in sin and guilt, unable to accept forgiveness.

2. Develop a regular discipline for yourself with regard to confession and forgiveness. This should include praying for yourself on a regular basis but also taking advantage of your church's ministry of forgiveness through services of confession and absolution, Holy Communion, and so forth.

3. If you have never done so, you might want to go through a formal rite of confession and absolution with your pastor. This will enhance your sense of the power of forgiveness as you minister to others through prayers for healing and forgiveness. In preparation for this service of confession, make an inventory of those things in your life that create a sense of guilt, fear, or resentment. Include such things as ways you have hurt others, resentments you feel because of being hurt, unresolved conflicts that cause you remorse or pain, ways you have broken God's law or have violated your own values.

Chapter Five

WHEN PEOPLE ARE NOT CURED

*Then the disciples came to Jesus privately and said,
"Why could we not cast it out?"
(Matthew 17:19)*

Can't you see the frustration on the faces of the disciples as they asked Jesus this question? Peter, James, and John had been on the mountain with Jesus and had witnessed his transfiguration. And while these four were away, a man came to the other disciples for help. This man's son was possessed by a demon, but the disciples could not heal the boy.

When discussing spiritual healing through the laying on of hands and prayer, the topic that raises the most questions and seems to raise the most fear is, What happens when people are not cured?

Often there is behind the question a very real and understandable fear that if a person is not cured, he or she will lose faith in God or question whether there is a God. The question might also reflect the pray-er's fear of losing face. But we do not pray for healing because we can guarantee a cure. We pray because we have been told to do this by our Lord, as a way to witness to the power of the Gospel to touch human lives. We pray in confidence that God hears our prayers and will answer them, even though we cannot predict what form that answer will take. The marvelous thing is that when we do what the Lord asks us to, the Lord will be present to bless.

Rather than face the possibility and consequences of a person not being healed, we might be tempted to avoid being involved in a prayer ministry for healing that requires direct contact with people. Indeed, many are willing to pray for a person anonymously as part of a prayer chain or group but hesitate to become involved in a face-to-face encounter with someone who needs prayers for healing. These two forms of praying for healing should not be set against each other as if one were right and the other wrong. Both are valid forms of praying for healing. But it is true that if we meet directly with someone in order to pray with him or her for healing, we will have to face the facts—people do not always experience an immediate cure, and people get worse, and people die.

No matter how we pray, the possibility that someone will not be cured makes it important for us to examine what that means, and how that affects the way we prepare for and carry out our prayer ministry. There are both theoretical and practical issues to resolve. How do we understand the nature of God's activity among humans? What do we do with the tension between our mortality and God's saving work? And how do we persevere in prayer, given our limited ability to understand the mystery of prayer? These concerns affect our expectations about what happens when we pray. In turn, our expectations will affect our ability to recognize and understand the various ways healing can be experienced.

Expectations and Healing

God is in control of what happens when we pray for healing. This means that we cannot determine the outcome of any prayer. This is not to say that we cannot expect anything of prayer. In fact, we can expect a great deal. With the conviction that God is in control of the healing, we can come in expectant faith to receive whatever God gives, confident that we come together because of God's grace revealed in Jesus Christ. This expectation creates a positive environment for healing to occur and yet allows us to be open to accept whatever might happen.

One of the expectations that many people have when they come for prayers for healing is that God will bring a total cure at that moment. Such a cure happens on occasion. However, most healing is a process that takes place over a period of time. Each time prayer is offered, improvement might follow. Therefore, it is often important that prayers for healing be offered on an ongoing basis. It is wise to counsel persons being prayed for that they continue to seek this healing ministry for an extended period of time and continue to receive the healing that God desires for them.

We would also do well to recognize and counsel those for whom we pray that there can be many outcomes to prayer for healing. And as pray-ers, because we do not know for sure what will happen, we simply remain attentive to what is happening. We remain attentive especially to the person for whom we are praying, so that we can assist him or her in understanding what might be happening, things that the person might not notice.

In almost all instances when I have been involved in prayers for healing, the person being prayed for has been made more whole in some way. Those prayed for speak of various ways they have been blessed, even if they have not received a cure in that moment. Especially when a cure does not happen, we might invite the person being prayed for to describe what did happen as a result of the prayer, so that he or she becomes more aware of the positive elements of the experience.

A person might experience a cure some time after the prayer session. We can encourage people to look for signs of healing in the next few days after they have received prayer. A woman came for anointing and laying on of hands for healing at a morning healing service. For some months she had been unable to use her right hand because of a weakness in her wrist. Someone prayed for her, and there was no immediate sense that her wrist was healed. The morning after the prayer, however, she was surprised that she was able to pour coffee with her right hand. Perhaps the more profound healing, however, was yet to come: She had been away from the church for many years, but following this healing experience, she came back into the church.

It might be that some people do not desire to be healed. They might request healing prayers and yet unconsciously not really want to be healed. The thought of being healed might be threatening to them. Being healed might require a change that they are not ready to make. They might have grown accustomed to being ill and be afraid to live without the illness. Or they might believe they need the illness to ensure they will receive attention from others and not be left alone. Or they might use the illness in some other way to help them cope with their lives.

This is a difficult and sensitive matter, perhaps one that will itself require healing before the presenting issue can be dealt with. If a person comes for prayer for healing and we sense resistance from the person, we might try to discern whether or not he or she really desires to be healed. If the person comes for prayer but never allows time to pray, seeming to prefer focusing on other concerns, we might need gently to help the person examine the role that the illness plays in his or her life and whether he or she is ready to be healed.

Jesus appears to have encountered a situation like this when he met the man at the pool of Bethzatha (older translations call the place Bethesda) who had been trying to get into the water when it was disturbed by an angel. The man had not succeeded in doing this for thirty-eight years. The text says, "When Jesus saw him lying there and knew that he had been there a long time, he said to him, 'Do you want to be made well?' " (John 5:6). While we might not be as bold as Jesus, this is a legitimate question that needs to be explored graciously when we encounter similar situations.

When persons do not receive a cure or their expected outcome, it is not helpful for us to begin seeking someone to blame. This is a human tendency that we all need to resist. While blaming someone—the one for whom we are praying, ourselves, others praying with us, or God—might provide some relief for the moment, it will not contribute in the long run to the person's healing. When we pray for healing, we will not always know why things are happening the way they are. There are many reasons God does not grant an instant cure—reasons we cannot know. We are, after all, dealing with the realm of mystery! But a wise prayer guide focuses attention not on blaming or explaining but on what the Lord *is* doing and revealing. We do not want to get lost in having to justify God or ourselves or to explain unknowable events. We can rather receive what God is giving with thanksgiving, affirm the person for whom we are praying, and keep the future as open as possible so that God may continue to heal that person.

Healing Prayer and Death

At times we may find ourselves praying for persons who are quite close to death. Either through an accident or a life-threatening illness, the person appears to be dying. In this situation it is appropriate to pray for healing. The prayers for healing on these occasions will include reference to the healing that comes through death and the gift of life in Christ that does not end. If the person dies, that does not mean our prayers have been in vain. Prayer always builds up the relationship with God and blesses—whatever its outcome might be. But we will all die one day. Even those Jesus raised from dead eventually died. We do not know why death happens when it does, but for the Christian, death is the doorway to the perfect healing.

We experience much sorrow and loss when a person who is important to us dies. We often find it difficult to let people go in death, seeking to hold on to them as long as possible. We might even deny that a person is dying. Praying in this situation requires much sensitivity. We do not want to get caught in denial and keep the one who is dying from the important task of preparing for death. Denial might be a problem for those who are close to the dying person, as well.

When we minister to dying persons and those who love them, we seek to help them deal with their emotions. People usually need to acknowledge and work through fear, anger, and frustration. These emotions can be expressed in the prayers that we share with the one who is dying and with friends and family. Sickness, illness, and death are real enemies. When we face them, we allow ourselves to work through the process of dying. We come to accept that the enemies are real and lay hold of the victory over them by Jesus Christ. Sometimes the victory will be celebrated in a cure, sometimes in the death of a believer who finds the Savior waiting with open arms. But the victory will always belong to God.

When praying for those close to death, we might discover that God is letting us know when to release the person to death. I was visiting an old friend who had spent many years in the ministry of healing prayer. He was elderly and his health had begun to slip. I would visit him and pray for him with anointing oil and laying on of hands. One day I came to minister to him. As I prayed it became clear to me that he was going to die soon. From that point on the focus of our time together was on his death. When we pray in such a situation, we will want to pray for the gift of discernment to know in which direction God is leading this person—toward a cure or toward death.

Living in Pain and Incompleteness

The suffering, pain, and illness we all experience remind us that we are living long after the Garden of Eden and have not yet arrived at the resurrection. We live with many tensions and paradoxes. Each day reminds us that we are not perfect, yet we are saints in Christ. Not totally cured, but healed. Not without sin, but forgiven. Beset by many enemies of our bodies and souls, but not overcome.

Every person lives with limitations—some more obvious than others. Not everyone who suffers experiences a cure through prayer, medicine, or other forms of healing. In one sense, none of us experience a complete cure for all time. Yet within the boundaries of life, we can be healed—made whole in Christ—so that we live in balance and harmony within ourselves. Some day, when we take our place in the heavenly kingdom, the boundaries of our lives will be expanded far beyond our imagination. Until then, we live with the struggle between what we are and what God promises we shall be. And we live with confidence that God does not leave us alone in our struggle. God promises to be with us and give us strength, courage, and renewal through the Holy Spirit.

When the apostle Paul prayed that God would take the "thorn in the flesh" from him, Paul heard that God would sustain him through grace, and that God's grace would be sufficient. In Romans we read, "We know that all things work together for good for those who love God, who are called according to his purpose" (Romans 8:28). Knowing and loving God in Jesus Christ does provide sustaining grace for those who suffer.

I have a friend who was born with cerebral palsy. For years he lived with a negative attitude toward himself, others, and God. He was caught in self-pity, anger over the frustration in his life, and an attitude that said, "I'll get you before you get me." Through the loving ministry of other Christians, he discovered his worth through God's grace. He became healed, not through the curing of his cerebral palsy but by the renewing of his mind and spirit in Christ. His story and many others have convinced me that what I have always believed is true: the deepest and most far-reaching healing is the healing of the spirit.

I do not know why some people are cured and others are not. I do know that God promises to be at work in everyone who desires to be made whole. Over the years I have prayed for healing, not all have been cured. But all have been blessed.

For REFLECTION *and* DISCUSSION

1. When you think about praying face to face with someone for healing, what fears or concerns come to mind? How do you respond to those concerns within yourself? Does the question of whether or not the person will be cured present a dilemma to you?

2. I met a man who was very angry at God and had rejected a relationship with God, because God did not heal his son when he prayed diligently for his son not to lose his eye. What would you say to this man about unanswered prayer and who God is? Was he wrong to feel as he did? Why or why not? Was he right to express his feelings the way he did? Why or why not? Is there a path of healing for the son and the father?

3. If you have offered prayers for healing and the person has not been cured, reflect on that. What was your experience? Can you share it with others?

ACTIVITIES

1. Read the book of Job. Explore how this book explains suffering. If you have a group to share with, discuss the issues in the book of Job that you have found to be meaningful. A commentary or study guide from your church library or a bookstore would be helpful.

2. Everyone is disabled at some point. What would you describe as some of the boundaries or limitations that hinder your life and do not allow you to be and do all you would like? Have you prayed about these? What happened when you did? Have you come to terms with these limitations in a way that says to you that you are healed? If you have not prayed for these limitations, take time to do so. Examine your feelings about these limitations. If these feelings are affecting you in a negative manner, pray for a healing of your attitude toward your limitations.

Chapter Six

HEALING PRAYER *in* *the* OLD TESTAMENT

"For I am the Lord who heals you."
(Exodus 15:26)

s the people of Israel made their way into the wilderness following their liberation from Egypt, God spoke these words through Moses to the people. God makes this promise to the people as a pledge in response to their obedience and faithfulness.

There are not many references to specific individual healings in the Old Testament, as compared with the Gospels and Acts. However, in the broad sense of healing, the Old Testament provides a clear picture of God seeking to renew and restore creation through the redemptive work being done in the Israelites. God's healing work is seen in great acts that free and sustain the people. Prophetic visions describe the healing of the nations through the word of God. Messianic prophecies project a future hope that God's chosen servant will bring healing of bodies, spirits, relationships, and all creation.

According to the Old Testament images, God is the one who will bring shalom—peace, harmony, and wholeness—to the world. Like a sign of hope for the world, God is at work in and through Israel with a redeeming purpose. God relentlessly pursues this people, cleansing, healing, restoring, and promising.

God Cares for the World

In the creation story, God looks with delight on the world that emerges from God's creative word. The world is good. Following the fall into sin and the brokenness and disharmony that come upon the world, God begins a long story of redemption and renewal. A pattern emerges in which God calls, gathers, enlightens, sustains, and renews people who will become a sign of this redeeming and healing process for the world.

A passage from the prophet Isaiah summarizes this picture of God's work in images that display God's love and concern:

> *But now thus says the Lord,*
> *he who created you, O Jacob,*
> *he who formed you, O Israel:*
> *Do not fear, for I have redeemed you;*
> *I have called you by name, you are mine.*
> *When you pass through the waters, I will be with you;*
> *and through the rivers, they shall not overwhelm you;*
> *when you walk through fire you will not be burned,*
> *and the flame shall not consume you.*
> *(Isaiah 43:1–2)*

This care of God is meant to enable Israel to become a beacon for all nations, to direct their attention to God, and to allow them to find God's salvation. Isaiah 49:6 paints another picture in which Israel is shown to be a light to the nations.

God's healing activity is not limited to human bodies, souls, and spirits. Healing extends to the whole creation. Isaiah 11 describes what will happen when God's messiah brings God's shalom for all creatures.

> *The wolf shall live with the lamb,*
> *the leopard shall lie down with the kid,*
> *the calf and the lion and the fatling together,*
> *and a little child shall lead them.*
> *(Isaiah 11:6)*

God's restoration reaches to all creatures, all that God has made. As prayers for God's restoring purpose, we will want to refer often to these passages in order to keep our vision as broad as God's—all things will be made new in the Christ, the Anointed One, the Messiah.

Individual Healings in the Old Testament

There are several individual healings in the Old Testament that bear witness to God's restoration. Those recorded tend to cluster in certain periods of Israel's history—the times of Moses, Elijah, Elisha, and Isaiah.

Several of the accounts of healing prayer related to barrenness. All of these stories relate to the birth of an important person. The first episode is found in Genesis 20: "Then Abraham prayed to God; and God healed Abimilech, and also his wife and female slaves so that they bore children" (v. 17). In Genesis 21 we also read that God healed Sarah's barrenness, as God had promised, and she bore Isaac. Samson was born to a woman who had been barren, after she was visited by a messenger of God who announced that she would conceive and bear a son (Judges 13:2-24).

Hannah was barren and prayed to the Lord when she visited the worship center at Shiloh. Her prayer was so passionate that the priest Eli, who stood nearby when she prayed, accused her of being drunk.

> *She was deeply distressed and prayed to the Lord, and wept bitterly. She made this vow: "O Lord of hosts, if only you will look on the misery of your servant, and remember me, and not forget your servant, but will give to your servant a male child, then I will set him before you as a nazirite until the day of his death. He shall drink neither wine nor intoxicants, and no razor shall touch his head."*
>
> *(1 Samuel 1:10-11)*

God heard Hannah's prayer, and she conceived and gave birth to Samuel. When Samuel was three, she turned him over to Eli to serve God, as she had promised.

There are four healing episodes related to Moses. The first involves healing Moses of leprosy. In Exodus 4:1-7 we read that God convinced Moses to lead the people of Israel out of Egypt. Moses asked for signs from God that he could share with the people, so that they would believe he had been sent by God. God told Moses to put his hand in his cloak. When Moses withdrew it, it was leprous. Moses was told to put his hand back in the cloak and take it out again. The hand was healed.

In the second incident (Numbers 12:1-15), Moses prayed for his sister Miriam. She was struck with leprosy after she and her brother Aaron spoke against Moses. Moses' prayer was quite brief and filled with passion: "O God, please heal her" (v. 13).

In Numbers 16:41-50 we read about Moses' and Aaron's act of prayer and repentance on behalf of the Israelites. The people had rebelled against Moses, and were struck by a plague as punishment. The prayer stopped the plague, after 14,700 had been killed. Numbers 21:4-9 records the more well-known incident of the poisonous snakes and the raising of a bronze serpent. The people had again rebelled against Moses, and God sent the snakes. The people repented and came to Moses and asked him to pray to God. Moses prayed to the Lord, and the Lord instructed Moses to lift the bronze serpent; anyone who looked at it was healed.

Healings are recorded as part of the ministry of both Elijah and Elisha. For example, Elijah restored life to a widow's son:

> *[Elijah] cried out to the Lord, "O Lord my God, have you brought calamity even upon the widow with whom I am staying, by killing her son?" Then he stretched himself upon the child three times, and cried out to the Lord, "O Lord my God, let this child's life come into him again." The Lord listened to the voice of Elijah; the life of the child came into him again, and he revived.*
>
> *(1 Kings 17:20-22)*

In a similar manner, Elisha brought life to a child who died. (This story is recorded in 2 Kings 4:8-37.) Elisha also healed Naaman, a commander in the army of the king of Aram (2 Kings 5).

A striking story of healing is recorded in Isaiah 38. Hezekiah, the king of Judah, became very ill and was at the point of dying. The prophet Isaiah came to him and told him to get his house in order because he was going to die.

> *Then Hezekiah turned his face to the wall, and prayed to the Lord: "Remember now, O Lord, I implore you, how I have walked before you in faithfulness with a whole heart, and have done what is good in your sight." And Hezekiah wept bitterly.*   *(Isaiah 38:2-3)*

The Lord sent Isaiah to Hezekiah with a message. "I have heard your prayer, I have seen your tears; I will add fifteen years to your life" (v. 5).

General References to Healing

There are several references to healing in the psalms. Some of them seem to refer specifically to overcoming illness. For example, we read, "The Lord sustains them on their sickbed; in their illness you heal all their infirmities" (Psalm 41:3).

Some psalms refer to the healing that comes from God to overcome a sense of judgment or abandonment. One psalmist wrote, "Be gracious to me, O Lord, for I am languishing; O Lord, heal me, for my bones are shaking with terror" (Psalm 6:2).

Still other psalms are strongly linked to forgiveness. Patrick Miller in his book *They Cried To The Lord*, says:

They are implicit, if not actual, prayers for forgiveness as well as healing, assuming a unity of body and soul, and believing that God is the one who "forgives all your iniquities, who heals all your diseases"(Psalm 103:3), who heals the broken of heart and mind as well as those with broken bodies (Psalm 147:3).[4]

The Old Testament prophecies that speak of the coming of the Messiah also contain references to healing. These passages describe a broad range of healing, from physical cures to a peaceful restoration of all creation.

Many of these prophecies are from the book of Isaiah. They point to the messianic age, when God's healing power will be manifested through the one whom God will send. For example:

> *Surely he has borne our infirmities*
> *and carried our diseases;*
> *yet we accounted him stricken,*
> *struck down by God, and afflicted.*
> *(Isaiah 53:4)*

These verses describe the Messiah as one who will suffer greatly himself, yet who through that suffering will provide healing and forgiveness for others.

Isaiah 35 describes in wonderful images the restoration of God, including physical healing:

> *Then the eyes of the blind shall be opened,*
> *and the ears of the deaf unstopped;*
> *then the lame shall leap like a deer,*
> *and the tongue of the speechless sing for joy.*
> *(Isaiah 35:4-5)*

In his opening sermon in Nazareth Jesus quotes this reference to physical healing and combines it with the opening verse of Isaiah 61:

> *The spirit of the Lord God is upon me,*
> *because the Lord has anointed me;*
> *he has sent me to bring good news to the oppressed,*
> *to bind up the brokenhearted,*
> *to proclaim liberty to the captives,*
> *and release to the prisoners …*
> *(Isaiah 61:1)*

Jesus claims these prophecies for himself as God's anointed one. His healing ministry is a part of God's plan for signaling the restoration of his creation. This plan, God's redemption of all peoples, continues to unfold in the New Testament and beyond, as Jesus sends his disciples into the whole world to preach, teach, and heal.

It is clear that we are called to serve this purpose of God as God's people. We are called—in continuity with God's people of all ages—to be a redemptive and healing community in the world so that all people may be drawn to God's salvation. The healing ministry of the church becomes one of the signs of God's care for all of God's creatures. It is one of the ways the redemptive work of God is made visible.

The Old Testament is a rich resource for our prayer journey. It covers many centuries of a people's physical and spiritual journey to come into their own place in God's plan. This is our journey as well. The Old Testament witness to God's healing activity encourages all of us to bring our needs to God with confidence. We learn from God's ancient people that healing activity is usual for God, that God hears our prayers, that individual healing plays a role in the healing of the whole creation, and that healing is strongly linked to forgiveness as a part of God's renewing and transforming work for the whole person.

For REFLECTION *and* DISCUSSION

1. In what ways is your thinking about healing prayer influenced by these Old Testament references?

2. How do you respond to the images in the Old Testament that describe God's shalom touching all things, including animals and the earth? How can your awareness of God's command that humans are to have dominion over (care for) the creation give you new insights into praying for the healing of the earth?

3. How have you specifically received God's care? What helps you identify certain experiences as being "the care of God"?

4. In what ways do you demonstrate your care of the earth? How can you pray so that you participate in God's ancient, yet present, purpose to heal the world?

ACTIVITY

Choose an area of concern you have for an aspect of God's creation—water, air, forests, animals nearing extinction, your neighborhood. Pray regularly for that particular part of God's creation. Be aware of any ways your prayers might begin to call you to action.

Chapter Seven

JESUS' HEALING MINISTRY

"What do you want me to do for you?"
(Luke 18:41)

J esus asked this question of the blind man in Jericho. Through it Jesus opened the door to the treasures of the kingdom for this man. He also allowed the man to ask for what has been on his mind every waking moment—if only he could see.

Jesus begins his public ministry by announcing, "The time is fulfilled and the kingdom of God has come near; repent, and believe the good news" (Mark 1:15). He proceeds to call disciples, to teach the multitudes, and to perform miracles of healing.

Jesus carried out his ministry in an integrated fashion. He did not only preach. He did not just offer forums for learning. He did not hold special healing services. Wherever people gathered, he preached, taught, and healed, as there was a need. Each aspect of his ministry related to a central concern: the coming of God's kingdom. His preaching was an invitation to draw near to God, as God had drawn near to us. His teaching illumined God's will for humankind. His healings were signs that God is breaking in to free people from oppression, disease, alienation, and evil.

Even though Jesus' ministry finds its central meaning in his cross and resurrection, we cannot ignore the significance of his healing miracles. This is particularly true because Jesus sent out his disciples to heal, as well as to preach and teach (Matthew 10), although the disciples did all these things in Jesus' name and by his authority and not their own.

In the Gospels, the healing miracles of Jesus comprise a significant amount of material. They are a primary source for us in understanding prayer and healing, and they teach many practical lessons to guide our own efforts to practice this ministry in Jesus' name.

Observations about Jesus' Healings

The range of diseases that Jesus healed is very broad. There seemed to be no limit to his healing ministry. Nothing was too small nor too large. He cured Peter's mother-in-law of flu (Mark 1:29-31) and raised Jairus's daughter from the dead (Mark 5:21-43). Jesus cured bodily afflictions, such as blindness, deafness, lameness, fever, epilepsy, dumbness, and leprosy.

Jesus also brought healing of the mind to many, creating thinking and attitudes that were life-giving rather than destructive to self or to others. For example, Jesus invited himself to dinner at the house of Zacchaeus, a tax collector. After Jesus spent that time with him, Zacchaeus went through a change in attitude. He opened his heart in generosity and pledged not to defraud anyone. In fact, he promised he would repay anyone that he had cheated. Jesus commented about Zacchaeus, "Today salvation has come to this house" (Luke 19:9).

Jesus also brought healing to the spiritual dimension of human life. Not only did he proclaim God's forgiveness in order to heal from guilt, he accepted and affirmed the poor and outcast, thus healing their shame and sense of alienation. At an even deeper level, Jesus overcame the power of Satan that oppresses and possesses the human spirit. His many exorcisms bore witness that he could and would deliver people from the power of the evil one.

Jesus' healing was available to everyone. He healed the rich and the poor, the young and the old. He healed Jews, Samaritans, Romans, and Canaanites. Jesus' healings were an expression of God's grace and mercy for the entire human family.

Through the actions of Jesus and his comments about various healings, we learn about the motives for Jesus' healing ministry. One of his motives was compassion. When Jesus encountered a funeral procession coming out of the city of Nain, he observed that the funeral was for a widow's only son. Moved with compassion, he stepped forward and brought the young man back to life (Luke 7:11-17). Jesus seemed to be deeply aware of the effects of sickness and illness and the power of evil to thwart human life, and compassion is spoken of many times in the Gospels as a motive for his entire ministry.

The miracles of Jesus were also signs that the kingdom of God was breaking in upon people and that God was taking the initiative to redeem and restore the creation. These signs were given not just as acts of mercy in and of themselves, although they were meaningful in that regard, but they were meant to engender faith. That is, they were meant to encourage people to look to God as their Savior. The Gospel of John points out this motive in the story of the raising of Lazarus. As Jesus was standing before the tomb, he prayed:

> *Father, I thank you for having heard me. I knew that you always hear me, but I have said this for the sake of the crowd standing here, so that they may believe that you sent me.* *(John 11:41-42)*

The result of the miracle is recorded in verse 45: "Many of the Jews therefore, who had come with Mary and had seen what Jesus did, believed in him."

Although related to this motive of rousing faith, Jesus' ultimate motive was that God would be praised and glorified. And indeed, many of the stories of Jesus' healings end with a description of the people praising God in awe and wonder as they sense the power and reality of God in their midst.

Jesus used many different methods in his healing practice. He was not a magician in the sense that he used a set formula of words or rituals. Sometimes he just spoke a word declaring the healing accomplished, and it was. Sometimes he used touch—laying his hands on a person. One time he used saliva and mixed it with dirt to make mud to put on the eyes of a blind man (John 9:6-7). Often he would tell the person to do something, and the healing would follow. This was the situation with the ten lepers (Luke 17:11-19). He told them to go to the priests to receive their clean bill of health. As they went, they were cured. The word of healing was sometimes spoken in the presence of the person, and at other times it was spoken when the person was far away. It seemed that Jesus did what was appropriate for each person and occasion. Each healing was individual in its character and application.

In this regard, Jesus often asked a question of the person before healing him or her. Again, each question seemed to be unique to that situation. These are questions that at times we might need to ask ourselves when we offer healing prayer, or to ask those for whom we pray:

> *"What do you want me to do for you?" (Luke 18:41)*
> *"Do you want to be made well?" (John 5:6)*
> *"Do you believe that I am able to do this?" (Matthew 9:28)*
> *"Who touched me?" (Mark 5:30)*

All of these questions seem to have invited the sick persons to express their faith, to commit themselves to the healing, and to further open themselves to a trusting relationship with Jesus.

When Jesus acknowledged faith and gratitude, he seemed to be pointing to the larger healing that was happening to people. To the woman who reached out to touch the hem of his garment he said, " ... your faith has made you well; go in peace, and be healed of your disease" (Mark 5:34). To the leper who returned to give thanks he said, "Get up and go on your way; your faith has made you well" (Luke 17:19). These examples point to the importance of affirming faith in those who seek healing and including prayers of thanksgiving when we pray for ourselves or others.

Implications of Jesus' Healing Ministry

As we read and study the healing ministry of Jesus, we become aware of the fact that these healings were not impersonal transactions. The persons seeking healing for themselves or others entered into a relationship with Jesus that was marked by trust and openness. Jesus also entered the transaction of healing as a person with compassion and concern for the whole person. We see again that prayer for healing, like all prayer, is a matter of relationship and not rules, regulations, or rituals. Undoubtedly, Jesus' manner with people contributed to this sense that a relationship was at the center of what was happening. We will want to generate this same sense of the importance of the person and the relationship we have with them as we engage in prayers for healing. We can put our whole person into the act of prayer and through our presence and actions communicate love, trust, and hope.

Another observation about Jesus' ministry of healing has to do with the issue of authority. Jesus healed with authority, just as he taught with authority. This authority was an expression of God's will and God's presence in that moment. In order to demonstrate that he had authority even to forgive sins, Jesus healed the paralytic brought to him on a stretcher. Jesus spoke directly to the issue of authority:

> *"Which is easier, to say to the paralytic, 'Your sins are forgiven,' or to say, 'Stand up and take your mat and walk'? But so that you may know that the Son of Man has authority on earth to forgive sins"—he said to the paralytic—"I say to you, stand up, take your mat and go to your home."*
>
> *(Mark 2:9-11)*

We also can trust that healing is God's will and pray confidently in the authority of Jesus' name. When the disciples returned to Jesus after being sent out to preach, teach, and heal, they were amazed that even the demons were subject to Jesus' name. They discovered the authority of that name to bring about God's will and power to heal and deliver. (As will be noted later, the apostles went out with that same sense of authority in Jesus' name to pray for and declare healing.)

When the disciples returned in joy because demons were subject to them in Jesus' name, however, Jesus reminded them of what was most important. He told them to remember that their names were written in the book of life and not to get caught up in their power to cure only. Healing serves the larger issue of relationship with God. That is the difference between cure and healing. When we pray for healing, we do not rejoice only in God's power to cure. Our desire is that the person become more connected to God in faith and gratitude—that the whole relationship be strengthened—as a result of the cure. When Jesus cured the ten lepers, we can sense his deep disappointment that only one of those cured returned to give thanks and experience a more complete healing. Jesus asks very pointedly about the nine who did not return. They were cured but did not, as far as we know, find a new relationship with God in Jesus, a deeper healing.

A thorough study of the healing ministry of Jesus is an important ingredient for preparing ourselves to engage in prayers for healing. (See For Further Reading, page 79, for possible study resources.) There is much inspiration, information, and direction provided in such a study. The healing ministry was such an integral part of Jesus' demonstration that God's kingdom was breaking in, that it would be a great loss if we did not claim such a ministry for the church today.

For REFLECTION *and* DISCUSSION

1. What do you think is the relationship between Jesus' healing ministry and the other aspects of his ministry?

2. What questions arise in your mind as you reflect on Jesus' healing miracles? What answers do you find in Jesus' healing miracles to the question, "Who is Jesus?"

3. Reflect on the three motives of Jesus' healing ministry described in this chapter. Think of them in relation to your own motivation to pray for healing. Are they similar or dissimilar?

4. Reflect on the relationship of compassion and power as you see it in Jesus' ministry. Would Jesus give the church compassion for the sick without also giving it the power to act in his name? Why is the presence of both compassion and power important in prayer for healing?

ACTIVITIES

1. Read the ninth chapter of John's Gospel. This is the most complete story of a healing miracle in the Gospels. It includes an extended description of the follow-up to a cure that became a profound healing. What insights do you gain for your own follow-up with those for whom you pray?

2. To develop a solid understanding of Jesus' healing ministry, undertake a detailed study of all the healing miracles of Jesus, listed in Appendix A (page 75). Some questions you can ask in such a study are: What was the disease made well? What was the role of faith in the situation? Who initiated the healing? How did Jesus perform the healing? Write in your journal about the insights you gain in this study.

Chapter Eight

HEALING *in the*
HISTORY *of the* CHURCH

"And by faith in [Jesus'] name, his name itself has made this man strong,
whom you see and know; and the faith that is through Jesus has given him
this perfect health in the presence of all of you."
(Acts 3:16)

ometimes the light of healing has burned brightly in the church, and at other times the flame has been low. Nevertheless, the ministry of prayer and healing has had witnesses in every age, and God has continued to hear the prayers of his people and to bless them with healing and wholeness.

Healing and Prayer in the Early Church

The Book of Acts tells us how the ministry and message of Jesus were carried on in the lives and ministry of the disciples. They preached, taught, and continued to heal. The community of believers expanded, and the message spread as missionaries were called to the far edges of the empire and beyond.

We read in Acts about many healings that happened through the apostles, particularly Peter, Philip, and Paul. As had Jesus, they healed a wide range of human illness relating to the body, soul, and spirit. They healed a man who had been lame from birth, restored sight to the blind, raised the dead, freed a girl whose owners used her in divination, and healed diseases such as fever and dysentery. Acts also includes accounts of large numbers of people healed by the disciples. As the disciples made their mission journeys, they ministered in words and deeds and with signs such as those Jesus performed, including healing.

Their prayer and ministry was marked by the authority they had in the name of Jesus. They prayed in the name of Jesus, healed by that name, confronted evil in that name, and faced death with joy and confidence in that name.

Ministering in the name of Jesus does not mean using his name in a magical sense. The authority of his name is given to those who believe—who are in a faith relationship with him. This is reflected in an incident recorded in Acts, when some who did not believe in Jesus tried to use Jesus' name:

Then some itinerant Jewish exorcists tried to use the name of the Lord Jesus over those who had evil spirits, saying, "I adjure you by the Jesus whom Paul proclaims." Seven sons of a Jewish high priest named Sceva were doing this. But the evil spirit said to them in reply, "Jesus I know, and Paul I know; but who are you?" Then the man with the evil spirit leaped on them, mastered them all, and so overpowered them that they fled out of the house naked and wounded.
(Acts 19:13-16)

In contrast, James 5 describes what appears to be a normal practice within the early Christian community. People who were suffering and sick were urged to "call for the elders of the church and have them pray over them, anointing them in the name of the Lord" (James 5:14).

In addition to healing through the authority of Jesus' name, the disciples carried on this ministry of healing through the power of the Holy Spirit. Through the body of believers, the Holy Spirit continues the ministry of Jesus by providing gifts that make it possible to pray effectively and minister in Jesus' name. In 1 Corinthians 12 the apostle Paul identified healing as one of the manifestations of the Holy Spirit in the life and ministry of the church.

The gift of healing is often accompanied by other gifts of the Spirit. When Peter and John healed the lame man in Acts 3, Peter seemed to know that the man would be healed. He did not specifically pray for his healing but announced it, and reached out to pull the man to his feet. Apparently the gifts of knowledge and faith supported this healing. When the text says that Peter "looked intently at him," this would indicate that something more was going on—as if Peter knew that the man could be healed that day. In faith Peter stretched forth his hand to lift the man, and he was healed. In Acts 16 the apostle Paul is described using another gift, discernment of spirits, to heal a young woman and free her from being used as a fortune teller.

Based on the disciples' relationship with the Lord and the Holy Spirit, they acted in expectant faith. Praying for healing is not only making requests. It is listening for direction from the Spirit and then responding to the prompting of the Spirit by using the Spirit's gifts to effect a healing. It is clear that the disciples of the early church took Jesus seriously when he promised them that the Spirit would come upon them and they would be doing works even greater than Jesus'. Notice that Jesus also promised the authority of his name:

> *Very truly, I tell you, the one who believes in me will also do the works that I do and, in fact, will do greater works than these, because I am going to the Father. I will do whatever you ask in my name, so that the Father may be glorified in the Son. If in my name you ask me for anything, I will do it.*
>
> *(John 14:12-14)*

There is one notable difference between the healing ministry of Jesus in the Gospels and of the apostles in Acts. In the Gospels there is no record of anyone not being instantaneously cured by Jesus. Among the apostles we discover several cases where an instantaneous cure did not occur. The apostle Paul mentions his "thorn in the flesh" and says that he prayed three times to have it removed. However, whatever it was, it was not cured. Paul sent Epaphroditus to Philippi because he was sick and very nearly died (Philippians 2:25-30). Paul also had to leave Trophimus at Miletus because he was sick (2 Timothy 4:20).

Prayer and Healing Since the New Testament

In the two thousand years since Jesus healed, there have been in the church both periods of decline and bright spots when prayers for healing were a part of the ministry of the church.

The Eastern church, represented by the Orthodox bodies, has a consistent history of anointing and praying for healing. However, in the Western church the practice of spiritual healing varies from one historical period to another.

In the time immediately following the apostles, there were several prominent church leaders who spoke of healing continuing in the life of the church. These include Justin Martyr, Tertullian, Origen, and Iranaeus. In their writings, we find general descriptions of healings occurring in Christian communities. One authority notes:

> *Perhaps the most interesting discussion of healing among the ante-Nicene fathers came from Iranaeus in Gaul . . . . In* Against Heresies *one of his telling points was that heretics were not able to accomplish the miracles of healing that Christians could perform. They did not have the access to the power of God and so could not heal.*

> *Iranaeus attested to almost the same range of healings as we found in the Gospels and Acts. All kinds of bodily infirmity as well as many different diseases had been*

cured. There is no indication that Iranaeus viewed any disease as incurable or any healing against God's will. Indeed the whole attitude he voiced was that healing is a natural activity of Christians as they express the creative power of God, given them as members of Christ.[5]

Origen, who lived from about 185 to 254, also spoke of the frequent activity of healing through prayer during his time. He described healings performed by Christians invoking the name of Jesus.

For by these means we too have seen many persons freed from grievous calamities, and from distractions of mind, and madness, and other countless ills, which could be cured neither by men or devils. Origen saw that the name of Jesus could bring about a complete change even in his body, by removing a diseased condition. "[6]

In his early writings, St. Augustine said that healing and other gifts of the Spirit were not for the times after Jesus. However, later Augustine changed his mind and began to affirm the healing ministry. He devoted one of the final chapters of his book *The City of God* to describing healing miracles occurring in his own diocese. He had begun to request that a record be kept of all the healing miracles.

This was done ... once I realized how many miracles were occurring in our own day and which were so like the miracles of old and also how wrong it would be to allow the memory of these memories of divine power to perish from among our people. It is only two years ago that the keeping of records was begun here in Hippo, and already, at this writing, we have nearly seventy attested miracles. "[7]

As the church moved into the Middle Ages, a negative attitude toward spiritual healing developed. First, sickness began to be interpreted as punishment from God. Therefore, praying for healing was getting in God's way. Second, the Roman Catholic Church made anointing a sacrament, Extreme Unction. That is, it was used only for persons in severe illness and at the point of death. (Since Vatican II, the practice has changed. A rite called Anointing of the Sick may be celebrated at any time a person feels need, such as before surgery or childbirth.) Making unction a sacrament also took anointing for healing out of the hands of the laity and clericalized and institutionalized it. In spite of this negative environment, healings were recorded by many persons, particularly in the monastic movement. St. Francis of Assisi has many healings attributed to him. Catherine of Sienna and Bernard of Clairveaux were very active in praying for healing.

In particular, there is strong documentation on the healing work of Bernard. Three friends travelled with him and kept records of their observations.

> *During a visit with Bernard to Germany in 1146-1147, the three companions compiled a daily record of some of his healings. They were assisted by selected persons who contributed their own observations. One of the accounts included the following commentary:*
>
>   *Eberhard: On that day I saw him cure three others who were lame.*
>   *Franco: You all saw the blind woman who came into church and received her sight before the people.*
>   *Guadricas: And a girl whose hand was withered had it healed, while the chant at the offertory was being sung.*
>   *Gerard: On the same day I saw a boy receive his sight.*[8]

At the time of the Reformation, several opinions prevailed concerning the effectiveness of prayers for healing. Calvin was a dispensationalist, which means he believed that healing and other signs of the New Testament were only for the time of Jesus and the apostles. He stated that these signs were no longer necessary to the proclamation of the Gospel and the spread of the church.

Martin Luther rejected praying for healing in his early writings and counsel. However, later in his life Luther encouraged prayers for healing and engaged in them himself. He prayed for a healing for his friend Philip Melanchthon and Melanchthon was healed. Other instances of Luther praying for healing are recorded in letters and other writings. He did not write about prayers for healing in his major theological works and doctrinal disputations. As he understood it, prayer for healing was a part of the pastoral work of the church, related to the personal and mystical expression of faith and not to doctrinal disputations. In a letter to a pastor he strongly encouraged prayers for healing and provided a method for carrying them out.

> *To Pastor Severin Schulze, Venerable Sir and pastor, The tax collector in Torgau and the councilor in Belgren have written me to ask that I offer some good advice and help for the afflicted husband of Mrs. John Korner. I know of no worldly help to give. If the physicians are at a loss to find a remedy, you may be sure that it is not a case of ordinary melancholy … . This must be counteracted by the power of Christ and with the prayer of faith. This is what we do—and we have been accustomed to it for a cabinet-maker here was similarly afflicted with madness and we cured him by prayer in Christ's name.*[9]

During the seventeenth and eighteenth centuries, rationalism prevailed in most Western circles. There was an emphasis on God as impersonal force who had set the creation in motion and sat by and watched it play out its life according to natural laws. There was little room in academic and cultural centers for a view of God that would encourage healing prayer.

During the nineteenth and early twentieth centuries, signs of renewal of the practice of spiritual healing emerged. In addition to individuals who became well known for their practices of prayer for healing, several strong movements in the church called attention to this practice. One of these movements was Christian Science, which although not strictly speaking orthodox Christianity, did raise the issue of healing in American society and the church. The second strong influence also came from outside the mainline churches. Pentecostalism began to spread across America and the world. Supported by its emphasis on spiritual gifts, including healing, pentecostals began to practice an aggressive healing ministry.

In recent years most denominations have explored healing and prayer. Many have published liturgies for healing services. The literature in this field has grown tremendously. (However, many congregations have yet to explore this field of ministry.) Several contemporary persons have provided leadership for the church as it rediscovers a ministry of prayer and healing. Some of these leaders include Agnes Sanford, Francis MacNutt, John Banks, Emily Gardner Neal, and Leslie Weatherhead.

In addition, in recent times several organizations and orders have developed to encourage the church to be more assertive in this ministry. One of these, The Order of St. Luke, provides training materials, literature, conferences, schools of pastoral care with an emphasis on healing, and local chapters that support this ministry. This interdenominational order is committed to encouraging the church to practice a more intentional ministry of prayer and healing.[10] It seems as though we are entering a period of time when this ministry is being revitalized in the church and given its rightful place alongside the ministries of preaching and teaching.

As with most written history, we have seen fragments from church leaders, theologians, and well-known persons in church history. What we do not have recorded are the stories of the thousands of common folk in every age of the church who humbly lived out their faith. No doubt there are more stories than we could imagine about their daily prayer and experience of God's mercy and love flowing to them in healing grace. Such stories certainly abound today. As I listen to the faith stories of the ordinary church member of today, I hear the remarkable tales of healing and salvation.

For REFLECTION *and* DISCUSSION

1. Dispensationalism regards spiritual healing as a ministry confined to Jesus and the apostles. Dispensationalists would say that after the apostolic age, healing was no longer a sign needed to accompany preaching and teaching. Have you been influenced by dispensationalism in your thinking about spiritual healing? How do you respond to this way of thinking?

2. Have you explored the spiritual gifts that might be a part of your experience as a Christian? Reflect on 1 Corinthians 12, Romans 12, and Ephesians 4 and define for yourself where you think you fit in the body of Christ.

3. Is the church today the same as the church in the Book of Acts? That is, do the authority of Jesus' name and the power of the Holy Spirit operate today as before? Do you experience prayer with such authority in the church today? What obstacles might block the church from claiming authority in Jesus' name and the power of the Holy Spirit in its prayer ministry?

ACTIVITIES

1. Study in depth the healing stories from the Book of Acts listed in Appendix B (page 77). Reflect on the form of the healings, the roles of the one praying and those receiving the healing, and the use of prayer in healing.

2. Explore in depth the history of healing in the church. Refer to the books listed in the For Further Reading (page 79) for suggestions. Make a special study of the history of healing and prayer in your own particular denomination. Examine statements on healing put out by various denominations in recent times.

Chapter Nine

PRAYING *for* HEALING

Are any among you suffering? They should pray. Are any cheerful? They should sing songs of praise. Are any among you sick? They should call for the elders of the church and have them pray over them, anointing them with oil in the name of the Lord. The prayer of faith will save the sick, and the Lord will raise them up; and anyone who has committed sins will be forgiven. Therefore confess your sins to one another, so that you may be healed. The prayer of the righteous is powerful and effective.
(James 5:13-16)

ames clearly urges in this passage that the church be a healing community. Prayer and healing are linked in the life of the believers and the community. Healing prayer can be practiced today through those called and committed to this ministry. But how do we pray for healing? This question can be answered with regard to prayer for ourselves and prayer for others.

Alfred Price, a pioneer in the healing ministry of this century, provides a simple pattern for praying for yourself for healing.[11] First, he advises, relax your body and mind and let the tension drain from you. Focus on scripture passages that create a sense of being cared for by God. Immerse yourself in the images of such passages as, "Be still and know that I am God," "God is our refuge and strength," and "Come to me, all who labor and are heavy laden."

Second, be open to receive God's healing presence. Concentrate your own spiritual awareness on God's life for you. Pray for what is bothering you and release it to God's care for you. Imagine God taking your burden from you or healing what is sick. If your situation is such that you have little strength or motivation to pray for your own healing, ask others to pray with you.

Third, give thanks to God for hearing your prayer and promising to bless you. Your prayer of thanks is an act of faith in which you express confidence in God's concern for you and God's desire to bless you with wholeness.

How do we pray when asked to pray for someone else's healing? There is no set formula or action that is prescribed, but there are some general principles and patterns that can be helpful.

Preparing to Pray for Healing

Remember that you are not preparing to heal someone. God does the healing. You are preparing yourself to be a channel of God's healing presence. You represent a physical presence through which God's healing presence and blessing may flow. Prepare to listen with compassion and receive the person for whom you are praying with acceptance and grace. Also, listen for and be open to God's leading in the prayer you will pray. Often an intuition for a certain prayer will come to you. Prepare to pray in faith and confidence.

Preparation might include a time of prayer for yourself. Pray for forgiveness for any resentments or actions that might be a barrier between you and others. Pray for openness to the other person. If there is anything about the other person that seems to block your accepting him or her, pray for that to be removed. Recommit yourself to the healing ministry with a prayer that affirms your desire to be an instrument of God.

Refer to Scriptures that will nurture and inspire your trust in Jesus. Look particularly at some of the healing stories of Jesus. (These stories are listed in Appendix A on page 75.)

If you are praying with others as part of a team, spend some of this preparation time together. You might want to pray for each other as well, before you pray together for others.

Occasions come when there is no time for preparation. This should not prevent you from praying. Enter into the prayer time with openness and expectation, relying on the ongoing preparation that grows out of your daily walk with the Lord.

Praying for Physical Healing

When you are asked to pray for someone's healing, your own spontaneous prayers, prayers from your heart, will certainly be effective. And such prayers will naturally be part of almost any prayer ministry. Following, however, is a general pattern for prayer for physical healing. It is not the only model but describes the elements of the prayers usually offered for healing, whether in a formal or more spontaneous setting.

- First, find out what the problem is. Simply ask the person to describe what is wrong. This is not a medical interview but a time to learn what you will be praying for. As the person shares what is wrong, be aware of any insights that come to you about the condition and other matters that might shape your prayer. As the person shares, observe him or her. Is the person nervous or relaxed? Desperate or confident? Is the person maintaining barriers to keep you at a distance? Is the person embarrassed to share?

Answers to these questions might indicate how to proceed. You might have to spend some time building trust with the person, assuring him or her that God cares about the illness, or that you are not embarrassed or intimidated by what he or she is telling you. You want to create as open an environment for prayer as you can.

You might want to ask questions for clarification, so that you understand the situation and the person. (Questions at any point in the time you are together do not disturb the healing process.) For instance, it would be proper to ask if recently there have been any unusual events in the person's life. Often emotional traumas or extended, deep stress can begin to produce physical effects. You will want to pray about the stress or trauma, as well as about the symptoms that might have been produced.

- Second, offer the prayer you feel is appropriate. You might include a prayer for the presence of the Holy Spirit; an affirmation of the person for whom you are praying as an object of God's love; a specific request to God for healing of the illness, disease, or situation causing problems; other prayers as you are led; and prayers of thanksgiving.

The prayers you offer may be accompanied by anointing with oil or the laying on of hands. Anointing with oil for healing has both biblical and historical roots in the church. Biblical references include Isaiah 1:6, Luke 10:34, James 5:14, and Mark 6:13. Historically, the oil bears a relationship to baptismal anointing, when the minister marks the sign of the cross on the forehead of each person baptized.[12] Anointing with oil is not required for healing, but it does provide a physical experience of touch and can provide encouragement when associated with the name of God. (Jesus often used such physical encouragement along with the word of healing.)

The oil used is olive oil. It may be set aside for this special use by a blessing prayer. When applying the oil on the forehead by marking the sign of the cross, you may say, "I anoint you with this oil in the name of Jesus" or "I anoint you with this oil in the name of the Father, and of the Son, and of the Holy Spirit." Or you may pray the following prayer while you anoint:

> *O God, the giver of health and salvation; as the apostles of our Lord Jesus Christ, at his command, anointed many that were sick and healed them, send now your Holy Spirit, that _____ , anointed with this oil, may in repentance and faith be made whole; through the same Jesus Christ our Lord.*[13]

Throughout history the church has held various positions about whether or not lay people may use oil. In the early church lay people did use oil. Currently most denominations allow and some encourage the use of oil by lay persons set aside for this ministry of praying for healing.[14]

The laying on of hands, as well as anointing, may accompany prayers for healing. This, too, is a tradition associated with prayers for healing in both Scripture and the history of the church. This act helps the one being prayed for identify with the one praying and can help the pray-er communicate a sense of empathy through loving touch. It is helpful when using the laying on of hands to ask permission of the person being prayed for, to make sure he or she is comfortable with that practice. Normally you lay your hands firmly but lightly on the person's head. If several are praying, others may place their hands on the person's shoulders as well.

- Third, observe what is happening during the time of praying. Does the person you are praying with react in some way? Ask questions about what the person is feeling and experiencing. Praying for healing is a living, interactive process. Try not to make it mechanical or magical.
- Fourth, provide some post-prayer suggestions. Encourage the person to continue praying for healing. Let him or her know that healing is a process and that he or she should continue with the process of prayer. You might suggest that the person return later for additional prayer from you or your group. Some people who regularly pray for healing for others have a card with a healing prayer on it that they give to persons with whom they pray. You might become aware of other needs this person has that could be helped by a counselor or a support group within the church. You could suggest these options. If a cure has occurred as you have prayed, encourage the person to go to a doctor to have it confirmed medically.
- Finally, if you make a personal commitment to continue praying for this person, do so. Put the person on your prayer list and pray for him or her as long as you feel led to do so, or until you hear that the need is gone.

Praying for Inner Healing

People will come for prayers for healing for emotional, mental, and relational concerns, as well as for physical ailments. Prayers for inner healing are based upon the assumption that Jesus is the same yesterday, today, and forever. Jesus was present to the past experience, even though unrecognized. Jesus is present in the prayer you are offering in the present moment. Remember that there is no part of the human person or the human experience that is beyond the healing presence of Jesus Christ.

Many times this type of healing prayer involves healing old memories that are still producing harmful effects in the person. The person might need to forgive someone who has hurt, abandoned, or disappointed him or her. These non-physical concerns, however, often manifest themselves in a variety of physical disturbances, such as being unable to sleep, anxieties, anger, and so forth, so it might not be immediately obvious that the need is for inner healing.

Once it has been determined that prayer for inner healing is needed, much of the pattern described above can be followed when praying. Prayer for these situations, however, often also involves going back to the original incident in the person's memory and reliving the situation with Jesus present to speak a word of love, encouragement, or forgiveness.

The process in this type of prayer begins with an interview, as above. When it comes time to pray, explain what you and this person are going to do. Pray for the presence of the Holy Spirit to guide the person's remembering. Pray for Jesus to be present and to protect you spiritually in this process. Encourage the person you are praying with to relax and not force any memories to come.

You might begin by referring to various times in the person's life, starting as early as conception and birth. Refer to a life period and then wait for a hurtful memory to emerge. If none comes forth, move on to the next life period, such as childhood, adolescence, young adulthood, and so forth. As each memory appears, offer a prayer recognizing Jesus' presence in that memory. Ask Jesus to heal that memory and provide the love the person needs to be able to forgive. Ask the person to visualize Jesus present then, and to receive what Jesus would have done in that situation.

This type of prayer might take a long time and extend over several sessions. However, it might involve just one session for a particular experience. Experiences of abuse or other victimizations may be prayed for in this fashion.

It is important that you experience this type of prayer for yourself before you pray for others in this way. After you have experienced inner healing, you will be free to enter fully into prayer for another without being distracted by your own wounds. In the process of inner healing, you open doors to rooms of the inner life that have often been closed for a long time. Behind these doors lie repressed reactions to experiences that have been painful. Often tears accompany these memories, but the freedom and joy that finally come often allow people to regain a wholeness in their lives.

Praying for Healing of the Spirit

Sometimes what needs to be healed is the person's spirit. The person might need to realize God's forgiveness, to experience a renewal of faith, or to be freed from the powers of darkness. If people make a confession or reveal that they struggle to believe that God forgives, remind them of the scriptural evidence that proclaims God's mercy, and declare their forgiveness according to what they have confessed. If they seek renewal of faith, pray for them to perceive anew the reality of God's love for them, and pray for a fresh filling of God's Spirit within them. If they are struggling with the forces of darkness or evil and feel oppressed in their spirit, pray for God's Spirit to bring light into all the dark places of their life and surround them with spiritual protection.

You may rebuke the presence of the evil one if you discern a negative or dark spirit's presence. You can address this evil directly in the name and authority of Jesus Christ, demanding that it leave. If you encounter a situation where a strong presence of evil is apparent, you should work with others and not alone in that situation. It would be helpful to work with someone who is practiced in matters of deliverance ministry.

Praying for Other Healing

There are other situations where healing prayers might be appropriate. You can pray for the healing of marriages, families, friends, and social situations. Several years ago there was a nurses' strike in our community. We held a healing service in the church for the nurses and the hospital administrators. The purpose was to pray for a spirit of reconciliation for both parties, so that there would be no lasting effects from the strike.

Prayers for healing aspects of creation are appropriate as well. The creation is not alien to our Lord. My wife and I have prayed for trees that have then been healed from life threatening disease. I was asked to pray for a cat that had cancer. (I prayed for the cat; the cat was cured and is still living after several years, growing gracefully into old age.) This might seem strange to many, but I believe we have let ourselves drift too far from the awareness that everything has come from the Lord's hand and that God wants all things to be made whole in our Lord Jesus Christ. Let us not become arrogant and think that we can somehow separate ourselves and God's love from all that God has made.

Varieties of Prayer Forms

There are various prayer forms that can be used in healing.
- A person is anointed with oil and a general prayer for healing is offered. This form is often used in public worship services.
- A team of pray-ers gather with a person for a longer period of time. The person is surrounded by the prayer team and they "soak" the sick person with their loving presence and an extended offering of prayers. Silent prayer may occupy much of the time, but oral prayers are offered as well. There may be several sessions of "soaking" prayer made available to the sick person. This prayer form is often used in critical situations, or when the illness is deep-seated or long and chronic in nature.
- The laying on of hands is used with oral prayers by an individual or a team.
- A group of people, not in the same location, agree to pray for healing for a specific person at a set time.
- A congregation gathered for worship prays silently for persons in need of healing.
- Extended inner healing sessions are held, including confession and forgiveness, prayers for healing, conversation, and counsel.
- Members of the congregation are encouraged to view their participation in Holy Communion as an occasion to pray for healing through the sacrament.

Praying for healing involves a continuous learning process. The learning comes by doing, and by observing other gifted people who have more experience with this ministry. As you offer intercessions for healing, you will continue to grow in sensitivity and skill, providing comfort for people as you communicate God's wonderful love, love that makes us whole in body, mind, and spirit.

For REFLECTION *and* DISCUSSION

1. Reflect on your previous experiences of praying for healing for someone. Do you know what happened as a result of your prayer? What was your reaction to the prayer experience?

2. Do you regularly pray for healing for yourself? At those times when you do pray for healing, what prompts you to do so? Do you find yourself praying out of panic and frustration, a sense of trust, or some other experience?

3. Reflect on the method or general progression of healing prayer suggested in the chapter. Is it one you can use comfortably? Why or why not? What would you change?

4. How do you understand the listening role in prayers for healing? What happens when you try to center yourself and be quiet before God?

ACTIVITIES

1. If you have not done so, explore contemplative prayer forms that will enable you to be more attentive and present both to God and the ones for whom you pray.

2. Ask your pastor to set aside and bless oil that you may use in anointing and praying for healing. When you are using the oil in a prayer situation, you may put it in a small glass dish; place it on cotton in a small bowl; or use a metal container with cotton in it called an oil stock, which can be purchased in a church supply store.

3. With a group at your church, practice praying for each other for health and healing on a regular basis. Develop forms for prayers for healing that you might use in the church, in homes, or hospitals.

Chapter Ten

A HEALING PRAYER MINISTRY *in the* CHURCH

These twelve Jesus sent out with the following instructions: "... As you go, proclaim the good news, 'The kingdom of God has come near.' Cure the sick, raise the dead, cleanse the lepers, cast out demons." (Matthew 10:5-8)

t is an encouraging sign that the question of healing through prayer has become of intense interest to the churches in many lands. Individuals and small groups have always been interested in this and practiced it. But it is something new that the church, the congregation, accepts it as a gift and a task from God that belongs to a normal and healthy congregational life." [15]

Prayer ministry can take many forms in a congregation, depending on the size and personality of the congregation. This chapter includes descriptions of a variety of healing ministry forms.

Getting Started

There are several areas of general concern to address when planning to offer prayers for healing as a specific ministry of the congregation. First, the ministry should be a ministry of the congregation. Often this ministry is associated with a particular person or group of persons. However, to ensure that the healing ministry continues beyond the tenure of a certain person, the ministry should be affiliated with a responsible committee or board in the congregation. This affiliation will also help communicate to both members and nonmembers that the ministry is part of the church's total ministry. Those who will actually pray for healing will be acting on the authority of the whole congregation. Officially recognizing that the healing ministry belongs to the whole congregation also makes it more likely that this ministry will take place when the whole congregation is gathered, such as during Sunday morning worship. Then the whole congregation can offer prayers for people and situations that need healing.

The whole congregation should be made aware of the nature of this ministry and the forms it will take in the congregation. This educational effort will also build interest in the ministry and perhaps lead some people to become part of the prayer team or to seek prayer for healing. The process of education and nurture should not be rushed. Members of the congregation might struggle with the concept of praying for healing, and congregation and prayer ministry leaders cannot assume that everyone will immediately respond positively. There might be many questions about spiritual healing that need to be addressed. Sermons, classes, and other forms of communication should be used to interpret your congregation's understanding of this ministry.

As you begin to discuss and explore this ministry, announce to the congregation that you are seeking people who feel called to pray for healing. Often church leaders find that a personal invitation is the best way to interest people in a new ministry. There are many ways people can be involved in this ministry. Some might desire to offer intercessions for those who will do the actual laying on of hands and praying. They become an important prayer support group. Some will feel called to do the actual face-to-face praying with people. Others might wish to participate in a prayer chain devoted to healing concerns. People will respond to the invitation—maybe only a few, but that is fine. Others will be drawn to this ministry as time goes on. As soon as possible, those who have accepted the invitation to be involved in this ministry should be introduced to the congregation and set apart for this ministry at a public service.

It would be wise to establish a program to nurture and encourage those involved in this healing ministry. Group members will want to study healing in order to gain encouragement and insight. A basic study of the healing miracles of Jesus would be important. Members of this group can also pray for one another and thereby develop experience praying for healing. Group members might also take time to share concerns, either about the prayer ministry itself or about personal matters that affect members' prayers. And finally, a support group will provide a way to bring in new persons and integrate them into the healing team.

At the same time as the prayer team is being established, thought needs to be given to the setting in which prayers for healing will be offered. A service for prayers for healing, particularly when offered in a public gathering of the congregation, will be received more readily if it is done in the same style, character, and mood as the congregation's regular worship. Because many people's exposure to prayers for healing has been through television, they might expect that prayers for healing will be nothing like prayers normally offered in their worship setting. Since prayers for healing are effective in every style of worship—it is not the form of worship, the style of music, the personality of the pastor, or the quality of the choir that determines whether or not healing occurs—it makes most sense to use a worship style that members are already comfortable with. I have seen people experience healing both in highly liturgical services and in very informal gatherings.

As part of the planning for a healing service, give some thought as to how people can be helped to feel comfortable asking for prayers for healing in a public setting. In some congregations, particularly small ones, people might be hesitant to come forward for prayers for healing. They do not want to become the object of speculation about what is wrong with them.

Do not be discouraged if people do not flock to the healing services. It might take some time to develop awareness and openness so that people will come for this ministry. Also, do not be discouraged if people do not let you know what happened to them as a result of the prayers for healing. Just as Jesus was thanked by only one leper out of the ten who were healed, you might hear few reports from people who have been healed. Sometimes people will let you know what happened a year or two afterward, sometimes not at all. Celebrate and give thanks to God for those who do experience healing and let you know.

Occasions for Prayers for Healing

There are many forms in which the public and personal ministry of prayers for healing can be offered in the congregation. As the ministry develops in your congregation, you will want to think about expanding the opportunities for prayer, as appropriate to your congregation and community. Possibilities for providing a ministry of prayers for healing include:

- **Special healing services.** Congregations often begin by providing a healing service at some time other than Sunday morning. Some offer these services on a weeknight, Sunday evening, or at noon. They can be held monthly, weekly, or in some other pattern, such as on the festival day of St. Luke (October 18). Congregations also hold healing services by request of members or others in the community.

Many denominations provide liturgies for healing services. Lutheran, Episcopal, Roman Catholic, Presbyterian, and Methodist worship books include such services. Usually a healing service includes hymns that focus on the care of God and the compassion of Jesus, a confession of sin and a declaration of forgiveness, scripture readings that focus on the healing ministry of

Jesus, a short meditation on a scripture passage that encourages faith and expectation, opportunity to anoint and pray for healing with laying on of hands; prayers of thanksgiving, and a blessing.

Within the healing service, there are a variety of ways to arrange for anointing or the laying on of hands. Persons might come to the front of the church, where healing teams pray for them. Healing teams can be stationed in several places around the sanctuary and pray for those who come to them. People can request prayers for healing by raising their hands while remaining in their seats, and then people sitting near them can offer prayers, or healing teams can come to them to pray.

- **Prayers for healing in the Sunday morning service.** Prayers for healing can be offered as part of the Sunday morning worship. On occasion, prayers for healing can be the focus of the morning service. People could be invited to come forward at a designated time to receive an anointing and prayers. People also could be encouraged to come for a general prayer for health and blessing if they do not have a specific ailment. Some churches offer prayers for healing in conjunction with the celebration of Holy Communion. They post teams of pray-ers at each end of the communion rail or at the side of the church. Then after receiving the communion elements, people who desire may receive prayers for healing by going to one of the designated spots. Opportunities can also be made available at the close of the service for persons to come to the front of the sanctuary or some other place for prayers.
- **Services in homes or public facilities.** Since people are not always able to come to the church, the congregation might make a prayer team available to hold healing services in homes, hospitals, or nursing homes, if that is needed. Team members would visit in the home or facility and conduct the healing service. In a hospital or nursing home, there might even be people besides family and friends, such as staff members, who would like to participate.
- **Special services at church.** The prayer team might invite people in the congregation to request a healing service at the church for them. All that is needed is a team of persons to pray and a specific time for the service.
- **Prayer chains.** A telephone prayer chain for those who specifically want to be intercessors for healing could be developed. Members of the group that prays for healing can be a part of the congregation's regular prayer chain or part of a separate chain.

Healing and Evangelism

When the church goes public with a ministry of healing through prayer, it makes a strong witness to the community. The signs of healing that Jesus and the early disciples performed often opened the door to sharing the gospel. In my own experience, the same holds true today. When the church is courageous enough to step out in faith and pray in Jesus' name for healing, people are attracted. Many come to our healing services who are not of the church. They have a need that is not being met. They come in hope that their illness, pain, and suffering might be alleviated. As they experience the praying community of the church, their hearts are open to experience God in a fresh way. When they are surrounded by a praying community that offers them an experience of God's love, they are drawn to Christ.

Offering prayers for healing to the community is a ministry that demonstrates the compassion of Christ. This ministry demonstrates that the church is walking in the footsteps of Jesus and is interested in the whole community's well-being.

For REFLECTION *and* DISCUSSION

1. How would you imagine prayers for healing being a part of the ministry of your congregation? What steps would need to be taken to begin exploring the possibility that your congregation will carry out this ministry?

2. Based on your impression, what does a public healing service looks like? How would such a service be conducted in your congregation?

3. How do you respond to the statement, "Healing prayer belongs to all in the church, not just to a few"? Do you agree or disagree with the statement? How would you explain this statement to someone?

ACTIVITIES

1. Visit a healing service at another congregation. Talk to the pastor and lay persons involved in the ministry, keeping in mind ideas that would help you develop a healing ministry in your congregation.

2. Interview members of your congregation to discover what their response would be if healing services were begun in the congregation. Identify their concerns, questions, and suggestions.

Chapter Eleven

LIVING *in* JESUS' HEALING PRESENCE

As you therefore have received Christ Jesus the Lord, continue to live
your lives in him, rooted and built up in him and established in the
faith, just as you were taught, abounding in thanksgiving.
(Colossians 2:6-7)

In this life we will never achieve perfect health. We will never attain perfect wholeness in body, mind, or spirit this side of the resurrection. While we are in the world, we will live with both sickness and health, doubt and faith, sin and grace. When Jesus ate with a group of tax collectors and sinners, the Pharisees criticized him. Jesus responded by saying, "Those who are well have no need of a physician, but those who are sick; I have come to call not the righteous but sinners" (Mark 2:17).

Jesus uses the analogy of sickness and healing to make the point that if we think we are healthy, we will not see our need for a physician. But if we understand that we are sick, we will seek help. His implication was that all are in need of forgiveness, and some recognize it, while some do not. His analogy applies to bodily and mental illness, as well as spiritual illness. If we deny our need, we will not seek a cure. But we all need healing of body, mind, spirit, and relationships—because we are not yet perfect.

If we deny that we have any need, we allow sin, sickness, despair, and death to control us. Doctors say that often people wait too long before seeking help, and they come when the condition is far along and harder to cure. It has been my experience as well that people come for prayers for healing as a last resort. Their spiritual or physical condition has deteriorated to the point where extended, persistent prayers are required. God can and does on occasion heal people in the late stages of illness in a quick, almost spontaneous manner. However, usually it takes some time for the healing to happen.

Why do people wait so long before seeking help? The biggest hindrances might be pride, doubt, or ignorance. I heard the story of a man who was reminded by his wife many times to fix a leaking faucet. He put it off until it got so bad he had to shut the cold water off. After a few days of this, his wife got after him again. He went to the hardware store and got supplies and tools and set to work to fix the leak, but it had gotten so bad that he could not fix it. Finally, he called a plumber, who came and repaired the faucet at considerable cost.

Perhaps the man thought he could take care of it himself. Another person might have been uncertain about how to proceed, or might not have realized that there was a serious problem. In the end this man did what he should have done at the beginning. This scenario is similar to what we often do with our sicknesses. We deny or ignore them, assuming we can handle them ourselves. Or we hesitate to act because we are not sure what can be done. Or we simply neglect to act because we do not think the problems are serious. But while we deny or ignore, doubt, or remain in ignorance, the one who heals stands ready to bless us.

We can live in a way that promotes health and wholeness on a daily basis. We can live in the healing presence of Jesus. When we are conscious of our needs and have learned that Jesus stands ready to be with us, there are many things we can do to allow the healing of Jesus to be a part of our daily lives.

The key to health is balance. Finding the proper balance between body, mind, spirit, relationships, work, play, and attention to the environment is important.[16] Many of our problems arise because we have not kept balance in our lives. When things are out of balance, our physical, emotional, mental, spiritual, and relational health can all be affected.

Here are a number of suggestions for maintaining balance and seeking ways to live a whole life in Jesus' healing presence.

- **Practice daily confession and forgiveness.**
- **Take care of your physical health.** Eat a healthy diet, get proper exercise, and balance work, rest, and prayer. Listen to and feel your body. Respond to its needs. When you are aware that something is wrong, pray for your body, focusing on receiving healing for whatever is ailing you.
- **Be aware of your feelings and respond to them appropriately.** Try to discern the source of negative feelings. Seek to respond to them with prayer. Give thanks in prayer for all things in your life. Gratitude will do amazing things for your emotional health.
- **Practice as much humor as you can.** Humor helps in a variety of ways to maintain a pattern of healing in our lives. We have a physiological response to humor: Humor makes our bodies release endorphins, which promote healing. There is a theological sense in which humor relates to healing as well. Humor enables us to not take things or ourselves too seriously. Humor helps us to unburden ourselves and let go of the sense

that the world depends on us to uphold it. Humor helps us remember that God is here and in control, and we only need to enjoy it.

- **Pray frequently for the fruit of the Spirit.** Can you imagine anything more healing in your life than to enjoy the full expression of the Spirit, as the apostle Paul describes it in Galatians 5:22-23.
- **Practice the presence of God.** Think particularly of God's goodness, faithfulness, steadfast love, compassion, and joy.

For REFLECTION *and* DISCUSSION

1. What part of you seems to go out of balance the most? Body? Spirit? Emotions? Mind? How does that imbalance manifest itself in your life?

2. As you think back over your study of prayer and healing, how have your thoughts and feelings about the subject changed?

3. How do you see yourself involved in a prayer for healing ministry? Praying with laying on of hands? Interceding for the prayer teams? Serving on a telephone prayer chain? Ministering in some other way?

ACTIVITY

Meditate on the Lord's Prayer as a healing exercise.

A. **Our Father in heaven,**
    Reflect on God's care for you. How have you survived to this point? Where does God's care manifest itself most for you right now?

B. **… holy be your name,**
    Spend some moments worshiping and adoring God. Let the majesty and glory of God envelop you and lift you.

C. **… your kingdom come,**
    In your mind, quietly survey the people and situations that surround you today. Look at them through the compassionate eyes of Christ. Where does the kingdom of God need to come for you? for others? Pray in faith for yourself and them.

D. **… your will be done, on earth as in heaven.**
As you relax in the thought that God has a will and purpose for you today, notice any place where you resist God's will. Try to discern why you are resisting at that point. Are you afraid? Is there a conflict between your desire and God's leading?

E. **Give us today our daily bread.**
Think of all your physical needs today. How is God satisfying those needs through gifts of people, the community, and your resources? Reflect on your physical self and how you are being responsible for the gift of your body.

F. **Forgive us our sins, as we forgive those who sin against us.**
Ask yourself, "Is there any resentment nesting anywhere within me? Am I feeling any distance from God because of sin? Any distance from others? Am I being tempted to take the path of vengeance against anyone in my imagination or in my actions?" What is the prayer that will bring healing to this part of your life?

G. **Save us from the time of trial …**
Are you facing temptations at this time? Do you resist following God's leading? Are you feeling overwhelmed at any point? Focus prayer on these situations.

H. **… and deliver us from evil.**
Spiritual warfare is often difficult for contemporary Westerners to comprehend and relate to. Seek to identify anything that is at work in your life that might separate you from God, the Christian community, or your commitments to walk in God's way. Acknowledge those struggles to God, and ask God to take them on for you. Pray for direction in strengthening your spiritual life.

I. **For the kingdom, the power, and the glory are yours, now and forever, Amen.**
As you reflect on this doxology, visualize letting go of the kingdom, the power, and the glory. Can you give them over to God? Can you find that comfortable place in yourself where you feel companionship with God, where you "let go and let God"?

HEALINGS *in the* GOSPELS

Individual Healings by Jesus

	Matthew	Mark	Luke	John
The nobleman's son				4:46-54
The man with an unclean spirit		1:21-28	4:31-37	
Simon's mother-in-law	8:14-15	1:29-31	4:38-39	
A leper	8:1-4	1:40-45	5:12-16	
Paralytic carried by four men	9:1-8	2:1-12	5:17-26	
Sick man at pool of Bethzatha				5:2-18
The man with a withered hand	12:9-14	3:1-6	6:6-11	
The centurion's servant	8:5-13		7:2-10	
Raising of the widow's son			7:11-17	
The demoniac(s) of Gadara	8:28-34	5:1-20	8:26-35	
The woman with an issue of blood	9:20-22	5:25-34	8:43-48	
Raising of Jairus's daughter	9:18-26	5:21-43	8:40-56	
Two blind men indoors	9:27-31			
Dumb man possessed with a devil	9:32-34			
Daughter of the woman of Canaan	15:21-28	7:24-30		
Deaf man with impediment in his speech		7:32-37		
Blind man at Bethsaida		8:22-26		
Epileptic boy	17:14-21	9:14-19	9:37-43	
Man born blind, sent to Siloam				9:1-41
Blind and dumb man possessed with a devil	12:22-24		11:14-26	
Woman bent double for eighteen years		13:10-17		
The man with dropsy			14:1-6	
Raising of Lazarus				11:1-44
The ten lepers			17:11-19	
Blind Bartimaeus	20:29-34	10:46-52	18:35-43	
Malchus's ear			22:50-51	

Healings of Large Numbers of People by Jesus

	Matthew	Mark	Luke	John
The crowd at Simon Peter's door	8:16-17	1:32-34	4:40-41	
Crowds, after healing the leper			5:14-16	
The crowd near Capernaum	12:15-21	3:7-12	6:17-19	
Sick people healed, following John the Baptist's question	11:2-6		7:18-23	
People in the crowd before the feeding of the 5,000	14:13-14		9:11	
The crowd at Gennesaret	14:34-36	6:53-55		
People brought to him before the feeding of the 4,000	15:29-31			
Crowds beyond the Jordan	19:1-2			
The blind and the lame in the temple	21:14			
Some sick people at Nazareth	13:53-58	6:1-6		

General Statements on Jesus as Healer

Healing all kinds of sickness and disease	4:23			
Healing every sickness and every disease	9:35			
All who touched him were healed		6:56		
Healing all who were oppressed by the devil				10:38

Jesus Heals through His Disciples

Sending out of the Twelve	10:1,7-8	6:7-13	9:1-6	
Sending out of the seventy			10:1-20	

HEALINGS *in* ACTS

Individual Healings by the Disciples

The man lame from birth	3:12—4:22
Paul regains his sight	9:10-19; 22:11-13
Aeneas the paralytic	9:32-35
Raising of Tabitha	9:36-42
The crippled man at Lystra	14:8-18
Girl with a spirit of divination	16:16-18
Eutychus restored to life	20:7-12
Paul healed of snakebite	28:3-6
The father of Publius (fever and dysentery)	28:8

Collective Healings

Many wonders and signs	2:43
In Jerusalem, many sick people healed	5:12-16
Stephen performs many miracles	6:8
Philip heals many sick people at Samaria	8:5-8
Paul and Barnabas work signs and wonders	14:3
At Ephesus, Paul heals the sick	19:11-12
At Malta, sick people healed	28:9

NOTES

1. Richard J. Beckmen, *A Beginner's Guide to Prayer* (Minneapolis: Augsburg Fortress, 1994), pp. 51-52.

2. Agnes Sanford, *The Healing Light* (St. Paul: Macalester Park, 1947), p. ix.

3. Larry Dossey, M.D., *Healing Words* (San Francisco: Harper San Francisco, 1993), p. 164.

4. Patrick D. Miller, *They Cried to the Lord* (Minneapolis: Augsburg Fortress, 1994), p. 108.

5. Morton Kelsey, *Healing and Christianity* (San Francisco: Harper and Row, 1973), pp. 150-151.

6. Ibid. p. 151.

7. Ibid. pp. 184-185.

8. Frank C. Darling, *Christian Healing in the Middle Ages and Beyond* (Boulder, CO: Vista Publications, 1990), pp. 141-142.

9. Bengt R. Hoffman, *Luther and the Mystics* (Minneapolis: Augsburg Publishing House, 1976), pp. 199-200.

10. The International Order of St. Luke, P.O. Box 13701, San Antonio, TX 78213, (512) 492-5222.

11. Alfred Price, *Religion and Health and Healing* (Irvington, NJ: St. Luke's Press, 1943), pp. 59-61.

12. Phillip H. Pfatteicher, *Commentary on the Occasional Services* (Philadelphia: Fortress Press, 1983), p. 104.

13. *Occasional Services* (Minneapolis: Augsburg Publishing House, and Philadelphia: Board of Publication, Lutheran Church in America, 1982), p. 102.

14. Pfatteicher, *Commentary*, p. 96.

15. Peder Olson, *Healing through Prayer* (Minneapolis: Augsburg Publishing House, 1962), p. 24.

16. See Howard Clinebell, *Well Being: A Personal Plan for Enriching the Seven Dimensions of Life: Mind, Body, Spirit, Love, Work, Play, Earth* (San Francisco: Harper San Francisco, 1992).

FOR FURTHER READING

Beckmen, Richard J. *A Beginner's Guide to Prayer*. Minneapolis: Augsburg Fortress, 1994.

Darling, Frank C. *Biblical Healing—Hebrew and Christian Roots*. Boulder, CO: Vista Publications, 1989.

Darling, Frank C. *Christian Healing in the Middle Ages and Beyond*. Boulder, CO: Vista Publications, 1990.

Dossey, Larry, M.D. *Healing Words—The Power of Prayer and The Practice of Medicine*. San Francisco: Harper San Francisco, 1993.

Glennon Jim. *Your Healing Is Within You—A Pastoral and Scriptural Presentation of the Healing Ministry of the Church*. South Plainfield, NJ: Bridge Publishing, Inc., 1980.

Gusmer, Charles W. *And You Visited Me: Sacramental Ministry to the Sick and Dying*. Collegeville, MN: Liturgical Press, 1992.

Linn, Dennis & Matthew Linn. *Healing Life's Hurts—Healing Memories through the Five Stages of Forgiveness*. New York: Paulist Press, 1978.

MacNutt, Francis. *Healing*. New York: Bantam Books, 1974.

MacNutt, Francis. *The Power to Heal*. Notre Dame, IN: Ave Maria Press, 1977.

Miller, Patrick D. *They Cried to the Lord—The Form and Theology of Biblical Prayer*. Minneapolis: Augsburg Fortress, 1994.

Occasional Services. Minneapolis: Augsburg Publishing House, 1982.

Olsen, Peder. *Healing through Prayer*. Minneapolis: Augsburg Publishing House, 1962.

Peterman, Mary E. *Healing—A Spiritual Adventure*. Philadelphia: Fortress Press, 1974.

Pfatteicher, Phillip H. *Commentary on the Occasional Services*. Philadelphia: Fortress Press, 1983.

Sanford, Agnes. *The Healing Light*. New York: Ballantine Books, 1983.

Sanford, Agnes. *The Healing Gifts of the Spirit*. New York: Jove Publishing, Inc., 1976.

Sanford, John A. *Healing and Wholeness*. Ramsey, N.J.: Paulist Press, 1977.

Sanford, John A. *Kingdom Within: A Study of the Inner Meaning of Jesus' Sayings*. New York: Harper and Row, 1970.

Sharing: A Journal of Christian Healing. San Antonio: The International Order of St. Luke the Physician.

Shleman, Barbara Leahy. *To Heal As Jesus Healed*. Notre Dame, IN: Ave Maria Press, 1978.

CONTACT INFORMATION

Author:

Richard J. Beckmen

c/o Speedwell Press

P. O. Box 131327

Roseville, MN 55113

Publisher:

Speedwell Press

P. O. Box 131327

Roseville, MN 55113

Email: nockleby@earthlink.net

Website: http://www.speedwellpress.com